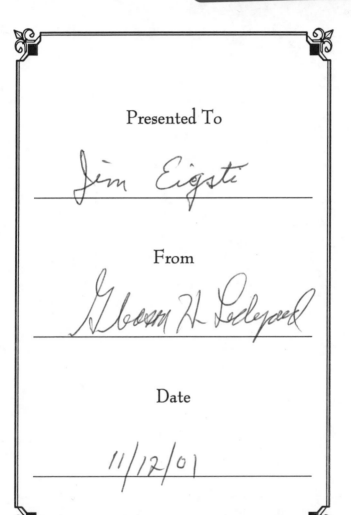

Presented To

Jim Eigsti

From

Glenn H. Ledyard

Date

11/12/01

Walking
In
New Life

Walking In New Life

...Then He will teach us His ways,
that we may walk in His paths...

Isaiah 2:3

New Life Version

Christian Literature International
P. O. Box 777
Canby, Oregon 97013

PREFACE

Walking is most often thought of as putting one foot in front of the other, thus propelling our body in a forward motion. However, there is another kind of walk that directly affects our manner, or behavior, or conduct. The Scriptures have much to say about this kind of walk. *Walking In New Life* was prepared to encourage the reader in his or her daily walk through life with the Lord.

Walking can be enjoyable when the path is smooth and our footwear is comfortable. Or it can be treacherous when walking on ice or loose stones in shoes too large or too small. Our daily walk in newness of life can be enjoyable if we are living in the will of God, or it can be miserable if we are disobeying God's Word and not paying attention to the Holy Spirit's leading.

Starting the day with Bible reading can set the right pace for our journey ahead. Come pitfalls or smooth going, Jesus Christ will sustain us and His Word will encourage us.

Walking In New Life can be read straight through as it logically follows the issues of life, or simply picked up casually and read. Reading a topic each day is a good guide for daily devotions. For a more in-depth Bible study, read the entire chapter from which each verse or portion is taken.

Walking In New Life uses the NEW LIFE Version text - the unique controlled vocabulary Bible.

Why not share an extra copy of *Walking In New Life* with a friend today?

Gleason H. Ledyard

For if a man belongs to Christ, he is a new person. The old life is gone. New life has begun.

II Corinthians 5:17

CONTENTS

UNDERSTANDING NEW LIFE

God's Word - Important

Keep these words (God's Word) in your heart that I am telling you today.

Do your best to teach them to your children. Talk about them when you sit in your home and when you walk on the road and when you lie down and when you get up.

Deuteronomy 6:6-7

This book of the Law must not leave your mouth. Think about it day and night, so you may be careful to do all that is written in it. Then all will go well with you. You will receive many good things.

Joshua 1:8

Happy is the man who does not walk in the way sinful men tell him to, or stand in the path of sinners, or sit with those who laugh at the truth.

But he finds joy in the Law of the Lord and thinks about His Law day and night.

Psalms 1:1-2

God's Word - Important

The Law of the Lord is perfect, giving new strength to the soul. The Law He has made known is sure, making the child-like wise.

The Laws of the Lord are right, giving joy to the heart. The Word of the Lord is pure, giving light to the eyes.

The fear of the Lord is pure, lasting forever. The Lord is always true and right in how He judges.

The Word of the Lord is worth more than gold, even more than much fine gold. They are sweeter than honey, even honey straight from the comb.

And by them your servant is told to be careful. In obeying them there is great reward.

Psalms 19:7-11

Your Word have I hid in my heart, that I may not sin against You.

Open my eyes so that I may see great things from Your Law.

O, how I love Your Law! It is what I think about all through the day.

Your Word is a lamp to my feet and a light to my path.

I love Your Word more than gold, more than pure gold.

The opening up of Your Word gives light. It gives understanding to the child-like.

Trouble and suffering have come upon me, yet Your Word is my joy.

All of Your Word is truth, and every one of Your laws, which are always right, will last forever.

Psalms 119:11, 18, 97, 105, 127, 130, 143, 160

The grass dries up. The flower loses its color. But the Word of our God stands forever.

Isaiah 40:8

"The days are coming," says the Lord God, "when I will send a time upon the land when the people will be hungry. They will not be hungry for bread or thirsty for water, but they will be hungry to hear the Words of the Lord.

"People will go from sea to sea, and from the north to the east. They will go from place to place to look for the Word of the Lord, but they will not find it."

Amos 8:11-12

Do not think that I have come to do away with the Law of Moses or the writings of the early preachers.

God's Word - Important

I have not come to do away with them but to complete them.

Matthew 5:17

Jesus said to them, "Is this not the reason you are wrong, because you do not know the Holy Writings or the power of God?"

Mark 12:24

Heaven and earth will pass away, but My Words will not pass away.

Mark 13:31

But these are written so you may believe that Jesus is the Christ, the Son of God. When you put your trust in Him, you will have life that lasts forever through His name.

John 20:31

Christian brothers, I want you to know the Good News I preached to you was not made by man.

I did not receive it from man. No one taught it to me. I received it from Jesus Christ as He showed it to me.

Galatians 1:11-12

Let the teaching of Christ and His words keep on living in you. These make your lives rich and full of wisdom. Keep on teaching and helping each other. Sing the Songs of David and the church songs and the songs of heaven with hearts full of thanks to God.
Colossians 3:16

You have known the Holy Writings since you were a child. They are able to give you wisdom that leads to being saved from the punishment of sin by putting your trust in Christ Jesus.

All the Holy Writings are God-given and are made alive by Him. Man is helped when he is taught God's Word. It shows what is wrong. It changes the way of a man's life. It shows him how to be right with God.

It gives the man who belongs to God everything he needs to work well for Him.
II Timothy 3:15-17

God's Word is living and powerful. It is sharper than a sword that cuts both ways. It cuts straight into where the soul and spirit meet and it divides them. It cuts into the joints and bones. It tells what the heart is thinking about and what it wants to do.
Hebrews 4:12

God's Word - Important

As new babies want milk, you should want to drink the pure milk which is God's Word so you will grow up and be saved from the punishment of sin.

I Peter 2:2

Faith - Necessary

O taste and see that the Lord is good. How happy is the man who trusts in Him!

The Lord saves the soul of those who work for Him. None of those who trust in Him will be held guilty.

Psalms 34:8, 22

You will keep the man in perfect peace who keeps his mind on You, because he trusts in You.

Isaiah 26:3

I am not ashamed of the Good News. It is the power of God. It is the way He saves men from the punishment of their sins if they put their trust in Him. It is for the Jew first and for all other people also.

The Good News tells us we are made right with God by faith in Him. Then, by faith we live that new life through Him. The Holy Writings say, "A man right with God lives by faith."

Romans 1:16-17

So then, faith comes to us by hearing the Good News. And the Good News comes by someone preaching it.

Romans 10:17

Anything that is not done in faith is sin.

Romans 14:23b

For by His loving-favor you have been saved from the punishment of sin through faith. It is not by anything you have done. It is a gift of God.

Ephesians 2:8

As you have put your trust in Christ Jesus the Lord to save you from the punishment of sin, now let Him lead you in every step.

Have your roots planted deep in Christ. Grow in Him. Get your strength from Him. Let Him make you strong in the faith as you have been taught. Your life should be full of thanks to Him.

Colossians 2:6-7

Faith - Necessary

He chose to make you holy by the Holy Spirit and to give you faith to believe the truth.

II Thessalonians 2:13b

Fight the good fight of faith.

I Timothy 6:12a

Now faith is being sure we will get what we hope for. It is being sure of what we cannot see.

A man cannot please God unless he has faith. Anyone who comes to God must believe that He is. That one must also know that God gives what is promised to the one who keeps on looking for Him.

Hebrews 11:1, 6

All these many people who have had faith in God are around us like a cloud. Let us put every thing out of our lives that keeps us from doing what we should. Let us keep running in the race that God has planned for us.

Let us keep looking to Jesus. Our faith comes from Him and He is the One Who makes it perfect. He did not give up when He had to suffer shame and die on a cross. He knew of the joy that would be His

later. Now He is sitting at the right side of God.
Hebrews 12:1-2

If you do not have wisdom, ask God for it. He is always ready to give it to you and will never say you are wrong for asking.

You must have faith as you ask Him. You must not doubt. Anyone who doubts is like a wave which is pushed around by the sea.

Such a man will get nothing from the Lord.

The man who has two ways of thinking changes in everything he does.

James 1:5-8

These tests have come to prove your faith and to show that it is good. Gold, which can be destroyed, is tested by fire. Your faith is worth much more than gold and it must be tested also. Then your faith will bring thanks and shining-greatness and honor to Jesus Christ when He comes again.

I Peter 1:7

Every child of God has power over the sins of the world. The way we have power over the sins of the world is by our faith.

I John 5:4

Need For New Life

The heart is fooled more than anything else, and is sinful. Who can know how bad it is?

Jeremiah 17:9

The Holy Writings say, "There is not one person who is right with God. No, not even one!

"There is not one who understands. There is not one who tries to find God.

"Everyone has turned away from God. They have all done wrong. Not one of them does what is good. No, not even one!"

Romans 3:10-12

Now we know that the Law speaks to those who live under the Law. No one can say that he does not know what sin is. Yes, every person in the world stands guilty before God.

No person will be made right with God by doing what the Law says. The Law shows us how sinful we are.

Romans 3:19-20

For all men have sinned and have missed the shining-greatness of God.

Romans 3:23

This is what happened: Sin came into the world by one man, Adam. Sin brought death with it. Death spread to all men because all have sinned.

Romans 5:12

You get what is coming to you when you sin. It is death! But God's free gift is life that lasts forever. It is given to us by our Lord Jesus Christ.

Romans 6:23

Preaching about the cross sounds foolish to those who are dying in sin. But it is the power of God to those of us who are being saved from the punishment of sin.

I Corinthians 1:18

But the person who is not a Christian does not understand these words from the Holy Spirit. He thinks they are foolish. He cannot understand them because he does not have the Holy Spirit to help him understand.

I Corinthians 2:14

Do you not know that sinful men will have no place in the holy nation of God? Do not be fooled. A person who does sex sins, or who worships false gods, or who is not faithful in marriage, or men who act like women, or people who do sex sins with their own sex, will have no place in the holy nation of God.

Also those who steal, or those who always want to get more of everything, or who get drunk, or who say bad things about others, or take things that are not theirs, will have no place in the holy nation of God.

Some of you were like that. But now your sins are washed away. You were set apart for God-like living to do His work. You were made right with God through our Lord Jesus Christ by the Spirit of our God.

I Corinthians 6:9-11

God's Plan For New Life

Jesus said to him, "For sure, I tell you, unless a man is born again, he cannot see the holy nation of God."

John 3:3

For God so loved the world that He gave His only Son. Whoever puts his trust in God's Son will not be lost but will have life that lasts forever.

For God did not send His Son into the world to

say it is guilty. He sent His Son so the world might be saved from the punishment of sin by Him.

John 3:16-17

For sure, I tell you, anyone who hears My Word and puts his trust in Him Who sent Me has life that lasts forever. He will not be guilty. He has already passed from death into life.

John 5:24

Jesus said, "I am the Way and the Truth and the Life. No one can go to the Father except by Me."

John 14:6

They said, "Put your trust in the Lord Jesus Christ and you and your family will be saved from the punishment of sin."

Acts 16:31

If you say with your mouth that Jesus is Lord, and believe in your heart that God raised Him from the dead, you will be saved from the punishment of sin.

When we believe in our hearts, we are made right with God. We tell with our mouth how we were saved from the punishment of sin.

Romans 10:9-10

God's Plan For New Life

For everyone who calls on the name of the Lord will be saved from the punishment of sin.

Romans 10:13

For if a man belongs to Christ, he is a new person. The old life is gone. New life has begun.

II Corinthians 5:17

For by His loving-favor you have been saved from the punishment of sin through faith. It is not by anything you have done. It is a gift of God.

It is not given to you because you worked for it. If you could work for it, you would be proud.

Ephesians 2:8-9

But God, the One Who saves, showed how kind He was and how He loved us by saving us from the punishment of sin. It was not because we worked to be right with God. It was because of His loving-kindness that He washed our sins away. At the same time He gave us new life when the Holy Spirit came into our lives.

God gave the Holy Spirit to fill our lives through Jesus Christ, the One Who saves.

Because of this, we are made right with God by His loving-favor. Now we can have life that lasts forever as He has promised.

Titus 3:4-7

This is the word He spoke: God gave us life that lasts forever, and this life is in His Son.

He that has the Son has life. He that does not have the Son of God does not have life.

I have written these things to you who believe in the name of the Son of God. Now you can know you have life that lasts forever.

I John 5:11-13

God's Forgiveness

But You are a forgiving God. You are kind and loving, slow to anger, and full of loving-kindness.

Nehemiah 9:17b

For His loving-kindness for those who fear Him is as great as the heavens are high above the earth.

He has taken our sins from us as far as the east is from the west.

The Lord has loving-pity on those who fear Him, as

a father has loving-pity on his children.

Psalms 103:11-13

O Lord, I have cried to You out of the deep places.

Lord, hear my voice! Let Your ears hear the voice of my prayers.

If you, Lord, should write down our sins, O Lord, who could stand?

But You are the One Who forgives, so You are honored with fear.

Psalms 130:1-4

"Come now, let us think about this together," says the Lord. "Even though your sins are bright red, they will be as white as snow. Even though they are dark red, they will be like wool."

Isaiah 1:18

He will crush our sins under foot. Yes, You will throw all our sins into the deep sea.

Micah 7:19b

All the early preachers spoke of this. Everyone who puts his trust in Christ will have his sins forgiven through His name.

Acts 10:43

Men and brothers, listen to this. You may be forgiven of your sins by this One I am telling you about.

Everyone who puts his trust in Christ will be made right with God.

Acts 13:38-39a

Because of the blood of Christ, we are bought and made free from the punishment of sin. And because of His blood, our sins are forgiven.

Ephesians 1:7a

God took us out of a life of darkness. He has put us in the holy nation of His much-loved Son.

We have been bought by His blood and made free. Our sins are forgiven through Him.

Colossians 1:13-14

Christ went into the Holiest Place of All one time for all people. He did not take the blood of goats and young cows to give to God as a gift in worship. He gave His own blood. By doing this, He bought us with His own blood and made us free from sin forever.

The Law says that almost everything is made clean by blood. Sins are not forgiven unless blood is given.

Hebrews 9:12, 22

God's Forgiveness

If we live in the light as He is in the light, we share what we have in God with each other. And the blood of Jesus Christ, His Son, makes our lives clean from all sin.

If we say that we have no sin, we lie to ourselves and the truth is not in us.

If we tell Him our sins, He is faithful and we can depend on Him to forgive us of our sins. He will make our lives clean from all sin.

I John 1:7-10

How To Know We Have New Life

For sure, I tell you, anyone who hears My Word and puts his trust in Him Who sent Me has life that lasts forever. He will not be guilty. He has already passed from death into life.

John 5:24

All whom My Father has given to Me will come to Me. I will never turn away anyone who comes to Me.

John 6:37

But these are written so you may believe that Jesus is the Christ, the Son of God. When you put your trust in Him, you will have life that lasts forever through His name.

John 20:31

Now that we have been made right with God by putting our trust in Him, we have peace with Him. It is because of what our Lord Jesus Christ did for us.

Romans 5:1

This is what it says, "The Good News is near you. It is in your mouth and in your heart."

This Good News tells about putting your trust in Christ. This is what we preach to you.

If you say with your mouth that Jesus is Lord, and believe in your heart that God raised Him from the dead, you will be saved from the punishment of sin.

When we believe in our hearts, we are made right with God. We tell with our mouth how we were saved from the punishment of sin.

The Holy Writings say, "No one who puts his trust in Christ will ever be put to shame."

There is no difference between the Jews and the people who are not Jews. They are all the same to the Lord. And He is Lord over all of them. He gives of

How To Know We Have New Life

His greatness to all who call on Him for help.

For everyone who calls on the name of the Lord will be saved from the punishment of sin.

Romans 10:8-13

But whoever obeys His Word has the love of God made perfect in him. This is the way to know if you belong to Christ.

I John 2:5

He has given us His Spirit. This is how we live by His help and He lives in us.

I John 4:13

I have written these things to you who believe in the name of the Son of God. Now you can know you have life that lasts forever.

I John 5:13

The Step Of Baptism

Those who told of their sins were baptized by him (John the Baptist) in the Jordan River.

Matthew 3:6

Be sorry for your sins and turn from them and be baptized in the name of Jesus Christ, and your sins will be forgiven.

Acts 2:38

Many of the people of Corinth who heard Paul became Christians and were baptized.

Acts 18:8b

All of us were baptized to show we belong to Christ. We were baptized first of all to show His death.

We were buried in baptism as Christ was buried in death. As Christ was raised from the dead by the great power of God, so we will have new life also.

If we have become one with Christ in His death, we will be one with Him in being raised from the dead to new life.

Romans 6:3-5

When you were baptized, you were buried as Christ was buried. When you were raised up in baptism, you were raised as Christ was raised. You were raised to a new life by putting your trust in God. It was God Who raised Jesus from the dead.

Colossians 2:12

The Step Of Baptism

Baptism does not mean we wash our bodies clean. It means we are saved from the punishment of sin and go to God in prayer with a heart that says we are right. This can be done because Christ was raised from the dead.

I Peter 3:21b

Freedom Through Christ

He said to the Jews who believed, "If you keep and obey My Word, then you are My followers for sure.

"You will know the truth and the truth will make you free."

John 8:31-32

So if the Son makes you free, you will be free for sure.

John 8:36

We know that our old life, our old sinful self, was nailed to the cross with Christ. And so the power of sin that held us was destroyed. Sin is no longer our boss.

When a man is dead, he is free from the power of sin.

And if we have died with Christ, we believe we will live with Him also.

We know that Christ was raised from the dead. He will never die again. Death has no more power over Him.

He died once but now lives. He died to break the power of sin, and the life He now lives is for God.

You must do the same thing! Think of yourselves as dead to the power of sin. But now you have new life because of Jesus Christ our Lord. You are living this new life for God.

Romans 6:6-11

At one time you were held by the power of sin. But now you obey with all your heart the teaching that was given to you. Thank God for this!

You were made free from the power of sin. Being right with God has power over you now.

Romans 6:17-18

But now we are free from the Law. We are dead to sin that once held us in its power. No longer do we follow the Law which is the old way. We now follow the new way, the way of the Spirit.

Romans 7:6

Freedom Through Christ

Now, because of this, those who belong to Christ will not suffer the punishment of sin.

The power of the Holy Spirit has made me free from the power of sin and death. This power is mine because I belong to Christ Jesus.

Romans 8:1-2

Christ made us free. Stay that way. Do not get chained all over again in the Law and its kind of religious worship.

Galatians 5:1

Christian brother, you were chosen to be free. Be careful that you do not please your old selves by sinning because you are free. Live this free life by loving and helping others.

You obey the whole Law when you do this one thing, "Love your neighbor as you love yourself."

Galatians 5:13-14

Happiness Through Christ

He began to teach them, saying,

"Those who know there is nothing good in themselves are happy, because the holy nation of heaven is theirs.

"Those who have sorrow are happy, because they will be comforted.

"Those who have no pride in their hearts are happy, because the earth will be given to them.

"Those who are hungry and thirsty to be right with God are happy, because they will be filled.

"Those who show loving-kindness are happy, because they will have loving-kindness shown to them.

"Those who have a pure heart are happy, because they will see God.

"Those who make peace are happy, because they will be called the sons of God.

"Those who have it hard for doing right are happy, because the holy nation of heaven is theirs.

"You are happy when people act and talk in a bad way to you and make it hard for you and tell bad things and lies about you because you trust in Me.

"Be glad and full of joy because your reward will be

Happiness Through Christ

much in heaven. They made it hard for the early preachers who lived a long time before you."

Matthew 5:2-12

Keep the faith you have between yourself and God. A man is happy if he knows he is doing right.

Romans 14:22

We think of those who stayed true to Him as happy even though they suffered. You have heard how long Job waited. You have seen what the Lord did for him in the end. The Lord is full of loving-kindness and pity.

James 5:11

But even if you suffer for doing what is right, you will be happy. Do not be afraid or troubled by what they may do to make it hard for you.

I Peter 3:14

If men speak bad of you because you are a Christian, you will be happy because the Spirit of shining-greatness and of God is in you.

I Peter 4:14

Humility Through Christ

God has given me His loving-favor. This helps me write these things to you. I ask each one of you not to think more of himself than he should think. Instead, think in the right way toward yourself by the faith God has given you.

Romans 12:3

Live in peace with each other. Do not act or think with pride. Be happy to be with poor people. Keep yourself from thinking you are so wise.

Romans 12:16

Are you strong because you belong to Christ? Does His love comfort you? Do you have joy by being as one in sharing the Holy Spirit? Do you have loving-kindness and pity for each other?

Then give me true joy by thinking the same thoughts. Keep having the same love. Be as one in thoughts and actions.

Nothing should be done because of pride or thinking about yourself. Think of other people as more important than yourself.

Do not always be thinking about your own plans only. Be happy to know what other people are doing.

Philippians 2:1-4

Humility Through Christ

In the same way, you younger men must obey the church leaders. Be gentle as you care for each other. God works against those who have pride. He gives His loving-favor to those who do not try to honor themselves.

So put away all pride from yourselves. You are standing under the powerful hand of God. At the right time He will lift you up.

Give all your worries to Him because He cares for you.

I Peter 5:5-7

The Believer's Hope

Hope never makes us ashamed because the love of God has come into our hearts through the Holy Spirit Who was given to us.

Romans 5:5

We were saved with this hope. Now hope means we are waiting for something we do not have. How can a man hope for something he already has?

Romans 8:24

Everything that was written in the Holy Writings long ago was written to teach us. By not giving up, God's Word gives us strength and hope.

Romans 15:4

Our hope comes from God. May He fill you with joy and peace because of your trust in Him. May your hope grow stronger by the power of the Holy Spirit.

Romans 15:13

Love takes everything that comes without giving up. Love believes all things. Love hopes for all things. Love keeps on in all things.

I Corinthians 13:7

We are waiting for the hope of being made right with God. This will come through the Holy Spirit and by faith.

Galatians 5:5

Our Lord Jesus Christ and God our Father loves us. Through His loving-favor He gives us comfort and hope that lasts forever.

II Thessalonians 2:16

The Believer's Hope

This truth also gives hope of life that lasts forever. God promised this before the world began. He cannot lie.

Titus 1:2

Now faith is being sure we will get what we hope for. It is being sure of what we cannot see.

Hebrews 11:1

Let us thank the God and Father of our Lord Jesus Christ. It was through His loving-kindness that we were born again to a new life and have a hope that never dies. This hope is ours because Jesus was raised from the dead.

We will receive the great things that we have been promised. They are being kept safe in heaven for us. They are pure and will not pass away. They will never be lost.

You are being kept by the power of God because you put your trust in Him and you will be saved from the punishment of sin at the end of the world.

I Peter 1:3-5

Living For Christ

For if a man belongs to Christ, he is a new person. The old life is gone. New life has begun.

II Corinthians 5:17

As you have put your trust in Christ Jesus the Lord to save you from the punishment of sin, now let Him lead you in every step.

Have your roots planted deep in Christ. Grow in Him. Get your strength from Him. Let Him make you strong in the faith as you have been taught. Your life should be full of thanks to Him.

Colossians 2:6-7

But the truth of God cannot be changed. It says, "The Lord knows those who are His." And, "Everyone who says he is a Christian must turn away from sin!"

II Timothy 2:19

As new babies want milk, you should want to drink the pure milk which is God's Word so you will grow up and be saved from the punishment of sin.

If you have tasted of the Lord, you know how good He is.

I Peter 2:2-3

Living Water

Jesus said to her, "Whoever drinks this water will be thirsty again.

"Whoever drinks the water that I will give him will never be thirsty. The water that I will give him will become in him a well of life that lasts forever."

John 4:13-14

It was the last and great day of the religious gathering. Jesus stood up and spoke with a loud voice, "If anyone is thirsty, let him come to Me and drink.

"The Holy Writings say that rivers of living water will flow from the heart of the one who puts his trust in Me."

Jesus said this about the Holy Spirit Who would come to those who put their trust in Him. The Holy Spirit had not yet been given. Jesus had not yet been raised to the place of honor.

John 7:37-39

For the Lamb Who is in the center of the throne will be their Shepherd. He will lead them to wells of the water of life. God will take away all tears from their eyes.

Revelation 7:17

The Holy Spirit and the Bride say, "Come!" Let the one who hears, say, "Come!" Let the one who is thirsty, come. Let the one who wants to drink of the water of life, drink it. It is a free gift.

Revelation 22:17

Obedience

Keep these words in your heart that I am telling you today.

Do your best to teach them to your children. Talk about them when you sit in your home and when you walk on the road and when you lie down and when you get up.

Deuteronomy 6:6-7

If you listen to these Laws and keep and obey them, the Lord your God will keep His agreement of loving-kindness as He promised to your fathers.

Deuteronomy 7:12

So be careful to keep the words of this agreement and obey them so all that you do will go well.

Deuteronomy 29:9

Obedience

I have put in front of you life and death, the good and the curse. So choose life so you and your children after you may live.

Love the Lord your God and obey His voice. Hold on to Him. For He is your life, and by Him your days will be long.

Deuteronomy 30:19b-20a

Samuel said, "Is the Lord pleased as much with burnt gifts as He is when He is obeyed? See, it is better to obey than to give gifts. It is better to listen than to give the fat of rams."

I Samuel 15:22

Anyone who breaks even the least of the Law of Moses and teaches people not to do what it says, will be called the least in the holy nation of heaven. He who obeys and teaches others to obey what the Law of Moses says, will be called great in the holy nation of heaven.

Matthew 5:19

Whoever hears these words of Mine and does them, will be like a wise man who built his house on rock.

The rain came down. The water came up. The wind blew and hit the house. The house did not fall because it was built on rock.

Matthew 7:24-25

If you know these things, you will be happy if you do them.

John 13:17

The one who loves Me is the one who has My teaching and obeys it. My Father will love whoever loves Me. I will love him and will show Myself to him.

John 14:21

If you obey My teaching, you will live in My love. In this way, I have obeyed My Father's teaching and live in His love.

John 15:10

Just to hear the Law does not make a man right with God. The man right with God is the one who obeys the Law.

Romans 2:13

We break down every thought and proud thing that puts itself up against the wisdom of God. We take hold of every thought and make it obey Christ.

II Corinthians 10:5

Obedience

The world and all its desires will pass away. But the man who obeys God and does what He wants done will live forever.

I John 2:17

We will receive from Him whatever we ask if we obey Him and do what He wants.

I John 3:22

Power Over Sin

Then I will put clean water on you, and you will be clean. I will make you clean from all your unclean ways and from all your false gods.

I will give you a new heart and put a new spirit within you. I will take away your heart of stone and give you a heart of flesh.

Ezekiel 36:25-26

What does this mean? Are we to keep on sinning so that God will give us more of His loving-favor?

No, not at all! We are dead to sin. How then can we keep on living in sin?

Romans 6:1-2

We know that our old life, our old sinful self, was nailed to the cross with Christ. And so the power of sin that held us was destroyed. Sin is no longer our boss.

When a man is dead, he is free from the power of sin.

Romans 6:6-7

Think of yourselves as dead to the power of sin. But now you have new life because of Jesus Christ our Lord. You are living this new life for God.

Romans 6:11b

Sin must not have power over you. You are not living by the Law. You have life because of God's loving-favor.

Romans 6:14

Christian brothers, now we know we can go into the Holiest Place of All because the blood of Jesus was given.

We now come to God by the new and living way. Christ made this way for us. He opened the curtain, which was His own body.

We have a great Religious Leader over the house of God.

Power Over Sin

And so let us come near to God with a true heart full of faith. Our hearts must be made clean from guilty feelings and our bodies washed with pure water.

Let us hold on to the hope we say we have and not be changed. We can trust God that He will do what He promised.

Hebrews 10:19-23

So give yourselves to God. Stand against the devil and he will run away from you.

James 4:7

My children, you are a part of God's family. You have stood against these false preachers and had power over them. You had power over them because the One Who lives in you is stronger than the one who is in the world.

I John 4:4

Rewards

You know that only one person gets a prize for being in a race even if many people run. You must run so you will win the prize.

Everyone who runs in a race does many things so his body will be strong. He does it to get a prize that will soon be worth nothing, but we work for a prize that will last forever.

I Corinthians 9:24-25

So then, Christian brothers, because of all this, be strong. Do not allow anyone to change your mind. Always do your work well for the Lord. You know that whatever you do for Him will not be wasted.

I Corinthians 15:58

Do not let yourselves get tired of doing good. If we do not give up, we will get what is coming to us at the right time.

Galatians 6:9

Remember this, whatever good thing you do, the Lord will reward you for it. It is the same to the Lord if you are a servant owned by someone or if you work for pay.

Ephesians 6:8

Crowns

It will soon be time for me to leave this life.

I have fought a good fight. I have finished the work I was to do. I have kept the faith.

There is a crown which comes from being right with God. The Lord, the One Who will judge, will give it to me on that great day when He comes again. I will not be the only one to receive a crown. All those who love to think of His coming and are looking for Him will receive one also.

II Timothy 4:6-8

Who is our hope or joy or crown of happiness? It is you, when you stand before our Lord Jesus Christ when He comes again.

You are our pride and joy.

I Thessalonians 2:19-20

A Christian brother who has few riches of this world should be happy for what he has. He is great in the eyes of God.

But a rich man should be happy even if he loses everything. He is like a flower that will die.

The sun comes up with burning heat. The grass

dries up and the flower falls off. It is no longer beautiful. The rich man will die also and all his riches will be gone.

The man who does not give up when tests come is happy. After the test is over, he will receive the crown of life. God has promised this to those who love Him.

James 1:9-12

When the Head Shepherd comes again, you will get the crown of shining-greatness that will not come to an end.

I Peter 5:4

I know of your troubles. I know you are poor. But still you are rich! I know the bad things spoken against you by those who say they are Jews. But they are not Jews. They belong to the devil.

Do not be afraid of what you will suffer. Listen! The devil will throw some of you into prison to test you. You will be in trouble for ten days. Be faithful even to death. Then I will give you the crown of life.

Revelation 2:9-10

GROWING IN NEW LIFE

Becoming A Full-Grown Christian

I pray that because of the riches of His shining-greatness, He will make you strong with power in your hearts through the Holy Spirit.

I pray that Christ may live in your hearts by faith. I pray that you will be filled with love.

I pray that you will be able to understand how wide and how long and how high and how deep His love is.

I pray that you will know the love of Christ. His love goes beyond anything we can understand. I pray that you will be filled with God Himself.

Ephesians 3:16-19

This is why I have never stopped praying for you since I heard about you. I ask God that you may know what He wants you to do. I ask God to fill you with the wisdom and understanding the Holy Spirit gives.

Then your lives will please the Lord. You will do every kind of good work, and you will know more about God.

Becoming A Full-Grown Christian

I pray that God's great power will make you strong, and that you will have joy as you wait and do not give up.

Colossians 1:9-11

God has chosen you. You are holy and loved by Him. Because of this, your new life should be full of loving-pity. You should be kind to others and have no pride. Be gentle and be willing to wait for others.

Colossians 3:12

Think about all this. Work at it so everyone may see you are growing as a Christian.

Watch yourself how you act and what you teach. Stay true to what is right. If you do, you and those who hear you will be saved from the punishment of sin.

I Timothy 4:15-16

Do your best to know that God is pleased with you. Be as a workman who has nothing to be ashamed of. Teach the words of truth in the right way.

II Timothy 2:15

Do your best to add holy living to your faith. Then add to this a better understanding.

As you have a better understanding, be able to say no when you need to. Do not give up. And as you wait and do not give up, live God-like.

As you live God-like, be kind to Christian brothers and love them.

If you have all these things and keep growing in them, they will keep you from being of no use and from having no fruit when it comes to knowing our Lord Jesus Christ.

II Peter 1:5-8

Practicing Self-Control

Josiah was eight years old when he became king. He ruled for thirty-one years in Jerusalem.

Josiah did what is right in the eyes of the Lord. He walked in all the way of his father David. He did not turn aside to the right or to the left.

II Kings 22:1a-2

But Daniel made up his mind that he would not make himself unclean with the king's best food and wine. So he asked the head ruler to allow him not to make himself unclean.

Daniel 1:8

Practicing Self-Control

Let every part of you belong to the Lord Jesus Christ. Do not allow your weak thoughts to lead you into sinful actions.

Romans 13:14

You know that only one person gets a prize for being in a race even if many people run. You must run so you will win the prize.

Everyone who runs in a race does many things so his body will be strong. He does it to get a prize that will soon be worth nothing, but we work for a prize that will last forever.

I Corinthians 9:24-25

But you, man of God, turn away from all these sinful things. Work at being right with God. Live a God-like life. Have faith and love. Be willing to wait. Have a kind heart.

Fight the good fight of faith. Take hold of the life that lasts forever. You were chosen to receive it. You have spoken well about this life in front of many people.

I Timothy 6:11-12

Take your share of suffering as a good soldier of Jesus Christ.

No soldier fighting in a war can take time to make a living. He must please the one who made him a soldier.

Anyone who runs in a race must follow the rules to get the prize.

II Timothy 2:3-5

Always Doing The Right Thing

Do for other people whatever you would like to have them do for you. This is what the Jewish Law and the early preachers said.

Matthew 7:12

Then Jesus stood in front of the leader of the country. The leader asked Jesus, "Are You the King of the Jews?" Jesus said to him, "What you say is true."

When the head religious leaders and the other leaders spoke against Him, He said nothing.

Then Pilate said to Him, "Do You not hear all these things they are saying against You?"

Jesus did not say a word. The leader was much surprised and wondered about it.

Matthew 27:11-14

Always Doing The Right Thing

Anyone who loves his neighbor will do no wrong to him. You keep the Law with love.

There is another reason for doing what is right. You know what time it is. It is time for you to wake up from your sleep. The time when we will be taken up to be with Christ is not as far off as when we first put our trust in Him.

Night is almost gone. Day is almost here. We must stop doing the sinful things that are done in the dark. We must put on all the things God gives us to fight with for the day.

Romans 13:10-12

You obey the whole Law when you do this one thing, "Love your neighbor as you love yourself."

Galatians 5:14

He who is taught God's Word should share the good things he has with his teacher.

Do not be fooled. You cannot fool God. A man will get back whatever he plants!

If a man does things to please his sinful old self, his soul will be lost. If a man does things to please the Holy Spirit, he will have life that lasts forever.

Do not let yourselves get tired of doing good. If we do not give up, we will get what is coming to us at the right time.

Because of this, we should do good to everyone. For sure, we should do good to those who belong to Christ.

Galatians 6:6-10

If you know what is right to do, but you do not do it, you sin.

James 4:17

Gifts Of The Holy Spirit

We all have different gifts that God has given to us by His loving-favor. We are to use them. If someone has the gift of preaching the Good News, he should preach. He should use the faith God has given him.

If someone has the gift of helping others, then he should help. If someone has the gift of teaching, he should teach.

If someone has the gift of speaking words of comfort and help, he should speak. If someone has the gift of sharing what he has, he should give from a willing heart. If someone has the gift of leading other

Gifts Of The Holy Spirit

people, he should lead them. If someone has the gift
of showing kindness to others, he should be happy as
he does it.

Romans 12:6-8

Christian brothers, I want you to know about the
gifts of the Holy Spirit. You need to understand the
truth about this.

I Corinthians 12:1

There are different kinds of gifts. But it is the same
Holy Spirit Who gives them.

There are different kinds of work to be done for
Him. But the work is for the same Lord.

There are different ways of doing His work. But it
is the same God who uses all these ways in all people.

The Holy Spirit works in each person in one way or
another for the good of all.

I Corinthians 12:4-7

But it is the same Holy Spirit, the Spirit of God,
Who does all these things. He gives to each person as
He wants to give.

I Corinthians 12:11

Christ gave gifts to men. He gave to some the gift to be missionaries, some to be preachers, others to be preachers who go from town to town. He gave others the gift to be church leaders and teachers.

These gifts help His people work well for Him. And then the church which is the body of Christ will be made strong.

Ephesians 4:11-12

God has given each of you a gift. Use it to help each other. This will show God's loving-favor.

I Peter 4:10

Fruit Of The Holy Spirit

I say this to you: Let the Holy Spirit lead you in each step. Then you will not please your sinful old selves.

Galatians 5:16

But the fruit that comes from having the Holy Spirit in our lives is: love, joy, peace, not giving up, being kind, being good, having faith, being gentle, and being the boss over our own desires. The Law is not against these things.

Fruit Of The Holy Spirit

If the Holy Spirit is living in us, let us be led by Him in all things.

Galatians 5:22-23, 25

Follow Instructions

So be careful how you live. Live as men who are wise and not foolish.

Make the best use of your time. These are sinful days.

Do not be foolish. Understand what the Lord wants you to do.

Do not get drunk with wine. That leads to wild living. Instead, be filled with the Holy Spirit.

Tell of your joy to each other by singing the Songs of David and church songs. Sing in your heart to the Lord.

Always give thanks for all things to God the Father in the name of our Lord Jesus Christ.

Be willing to help and care for each other because of Christ. By doing this, you honor Christ.

Ephesians 5:15-21

Be glad you can do the things you should be doing. Do all things without arguing and talking about how you wish you did not have to do them.

In that way, you can prove yourselves to be without blame. You are God's children and no one can talk against you, even in a sin-loving and sin-sick world. You are to shine as lights among the sinful people of this world.

Take a strong hold on the Word of Life. Then when Christ comes again, I will be happy that I did not work with you for nothing.

Even if I give my life as a gift on the altar to God for you, I am glad and share this joy with you.

You must be happy and share your joy with me also.
Philippians 2:14-18

God wants you to be holy. You must keep away from sex sins.

God wants each of you to use his body in the right way by keeping it holy and by respecting it.

You should not use it to please your own desires like the people who do not know God.

No man should do wrong to his Christian brother in anything. The Lord will punish a person who does. I have told you this before.

For God has not called us to live in sin. He has

Follow Instructions

called us to live a holy life.

The one who turns away from this teaching does not turn away from man, but from God. It is God Who has given us His Holy Spirit.

I Thessalonians 4:3-8

Prayer And Fasting

Let the words of my mouth and the thoughts of my heart be pleasing in Your eyes, O Lord, my Rock and the One Who saves me.

Psalms 19:14

When you pray, do not be as those who pretend to be someone they are not. They love to stand and pray in the places of worship or in the streets so people can see them. For sure, I tell you, they have all the reward they are going to get.

When you pray, go into a room by yourself. After you have shut the door, pray to your Father Who is in secret. Then your Father Who sees in secret will reward you.

When you pray, do not say the same thing over and

over again making long prayers like the people who do not know God. They think they are heard because their prayers are long.

Do not be like them. Your Father knows what you need before you ask Him.

Matthew 6:5-8

When you go without food so you can pray better, do not be as those who pretend to be someone they are not. They make themselves look sad so people will see they are going without food. For sure, I tell you, they have all the reward they are going to get.

When you go without food so you can pray better, put oil on your head and wash your face.

Then nobody knows you are going without food. Then your Father Who sees in secret will reward you.

Matthew 6:16-18

Ask, and what you are asking for will be given to you. Look, and what you are looking for you will find. Knock, and the door you are knocking on will be opened to you.

Everyone who asks receives what he asks for. Everyone who looks finds what he is looking for. Everyone who knocks has the door opened to him.

What man among you would give his son a stone if

Prayer And Fasting

he should ask for bread?

Or if he asks for a fish, would he give him a snake?

You are bad and you know how to give good things to your children. How much more will your Father in heaven give good things to those who ask Him?

Matthew 7:7-11

All things you ask for in prayer, you will receive if you have faith.

Matthew 21:22

When Jesus went into the house, His followers asked Him when He was alone, "Why could we not put out the demon?"

He said to them, "The only way this kind of demon is put out is by prayer and by going without food so you can pray better."

Mark 9:28-29

Whatever you ask in My name, I will do it so the shining-greatness of the Father may be seen in the Son.

Yes, if you ask anything in My name, I will do it.

John 14:13-14

If you get your life from Me and My Words live in you, ask whatever you want. It will be done for you.
John 15:7

In every church they chose leaders for them. They went without food during that time so they could pray better. Paul and Barnabas prayed for the leaders, giving them over to the Lord in Whom they believed.
Acts 14:23

You must pray at all times as the Holy Spirit leads you to pray. Pray for the things that are needed. You must watch and keep on praying. Remember to pray for all Christians.

Pray for me also. Pray that I might open my mouth without fear. Pray that I will use the right words to preach that which is hard to understand in the Good News.

Ephesians 6:18-19

We have a great Religious Leader Who has made the way for man to go to God. He is Jesus, the Son of God, Who has gone to heaven to be with God. Let us keep our trust in Jesus Christ.

Our Religious Leader understands how weak we are. Christ was tempted in every way we are tempted, but

Prayer And Fasting

He did not sin.

Let us go with complete trust to the throne of God. We will receive His loving-kindness and have His loving-favor to help us whenever we need it.

Hebrews 4:14-16

Tell your sins to each other. And pray for each other so you may be healed. The prayer from the heart of a man right with God has much power.

Elijah was a man as we are. He prayed that it might not rain. It did not rain on the earth for three and one-half years.

Then he prayed again that it would rain. It rained much and the fields of the earth gave fruit.

James 5:16-18

We are sure that if we ask anything that He wants us to have, He will hear us.

If we are sure He hears us when we ask, we can be sure He will give us what we ask for.

I John 5:14-15

Power Over Temptation

Watch and pray so that you will not be tempted. Man's spirit is willing, but the body does not have the power to do it.

Matthew 26:41

You have never been tempted to sin in any different way than other people. God is faithful. He will not allow you to be tempted more than you can take. But when you are tempted, He will make a way for you to keep from falling into sin.

I Corinthians 10:13

I am sure that God Who began the good work in you will keep on working in you until the day Jesus Christ comes again.

I pray that you will know what is the best. I pray that you will be true and without blame until the day Christ comes again.

Philippians 1:6, 10

And we sent Timothy to you. He works with us for God, teaching the Good News of Christ. We sent him to give strength and comfort to your faith.

We do not want anyone to give up because of trou-

Power Over Temptation

bles. You know that we can expect troubles.

I Thessalonians 3:2-3

So give yourselves to God. Stand against the devil and he will run away from you.

James 4:7

But the Lord knows how to help men who are right with God when they are tempted.

II Peter 2:9a

My children, you are a part of God's family. You have stood against these false preachers and had power over them. You had power over them because the One Who lives in you is stronger than the one who is in the world.

I John 4:4

Praise And Worship

Jesus said to the devil, "Get away, Satan. It is written, 'You must worship the Lord your God. You must obey Him only.' "

Matthew 4:10

The woman said to Him, "Sir, I think You are a person Who speaks for God.

"Our early fathers worshiped on this mountain. You Jews say Jerusalem is the place where men should worship."

Jesus said to her, "Woman, believe Me. The time is coming when you will not worship the Father on this mountain or in Jerusalem.

"You people do not know what you worship. We Jews know what we worship. It is through the Jews that men are saved from the punishment of their sins.

"The time is coming, yes, it is here now, when the true worshipers will worship the Father in spirit and in truth. The Father wants that kind of worshipers.

"God is Spirit. Those who worship Him must worship Him in spirit and in truth."

John 4:19-24

Tell of your joy to each other by singing the Songs of David and church songs. Sing in your heart to the Lord.

Ephesians 5:19

Be full of joy always because you belong to the Lord. Again I say, be full of joy!

Praise And Worship

Let all people see how gentle you are. The Lord is coming again soon.

Do not worry. Learn to pray about everything. Give thanks to God as you ask Him for what you need.

Philippians 4:4-6

Let the peace of Christ have power over your hearts. You were chosen as a part of His body. Always be thankful.

Let the teaching of Christ and His words keep on living in you. These make your lives rich and full of wisdom. Keep on teaching and helping each other. Sing the Songs of David and the church songs and the songs of heaven with hearts full of thanks to God.

Whatever you say or do, do it in the name of the Lord Jesus. Give thanks to God the Father through the Lord Jesus.

Colossians 3:15-17

In everything give thanks. This is what God wants you to do because of Christ Jesus.

I Thessalonians 5:18

Let us give thanks all the time to God through Jesus Christ. Our gift to Him is to give thanks. Our lips should always give thanks to His name.

Hebrews 13:15

With this hope you can be happy even if you need to have sorrow and all kinds of tests for awhile.

These tests have come to prove your faith and to show that it is good. Gold, which can be destroyed, is tested by fire. Your faith is worth much more than gold and it must be tested also. Then your faith will bring thanks and shining-greatness and honor to Jesus Christ when He comes again.

I Peter 1:6-7

It was I, John, who heard and saw these things. Then I got down at the feet of the angel who showed me these things. I was going to worship him.

But he said to me, "No! You must not do that. I am a servant together with you and with your Christian brothers and the early preachers and with all those who obey the words in this Book. You must worship God!"

Revelation 22:8-9

Studying And Teaching

These Jews were more willing to understand than those in the city of Thessalonica. They were glad to hear the Word of God, and they looked into the Holy Writings to see if those things were true.

Acts 17:11

Yes, I know that when I am gone, hungry wolves will come in among you. They will try to destroy the church.

Also men from your own group will begin to teach things that are not true. They will get men to follow them.

I say again, keep watching! Remember that for three years I taught everyone of you night and day, even with tears.

Acts 20:29-31

Do your best to know that God is pleased with you. Be as a workman who has nothing to be ashamed of. Teach the words of truth in the right way.

II Timothy 2:15

But as for you, hold on to what you have learned and know to be true. Remember where you learned them.

You have known the Holy Writings since you were a child. They are able to give you wisdom that leads to being saved from the punishment of sin by putting your trust in Christ Jesus.

All the Holy Writings are God-given and are made alive by Him. Man is helped when he is taught God's Word. It shows what is wrong. It changes the way of a man's life. It shows him how to be right with God.

It gives the man who belongs to God everything he needs to work well for Him.

II Timothy 3:14-17

God's Word is living and powerful. It is sharper than a sword that cuts both ways. It cuts straight into where the soul and spirit meet and it divides them. It cuts into the joints and bones. It tells what the heart is thinking about and what it wants to do.

No one can hide from God. His eyes see everything we do. We must give an answer to God for what we have done.

Hebrews 4:12-13

As new babies want milk, you should want to drink the pure milk which is God's Word so you will grow up and be saved from the punishment of sin.

If you have tasted of the Lord, you know how good He is.

I Peter 2:2-3

REACHING OUT WITH NEW LIFE

Sharing The Good News

Let your light shine in front of men. Then they will see the good things you do and will honor your Father Who is in heaven.

Matthew 5:16

Also, I tell you, everyone who makes Me known to men, the Son of Man will make him known to the angels of God.

But whoever acts as if he does not know Me and does not make Me known to men, he will not be spoken of to the angels of God.

Luke 12:8-9

I am not ashamed of the Good News. It is the power of God. It is the way He saves men from the punishment of their sins if they put their trust in Him. It is for the Jew first and for all other people also.

The Good News tells us we are made right with God by faith in Him. Then, by faith we live that new

Sharing The Good News

life through Him. The Holy Writings say, "A man right with God lives by faith."

Romans 1:16-17

All this comes from God. He is the One Who brought us to Himself when we hated Him. He did this through Christ. Then He gave us the work of bringing others to Him.

God was in Christ. He was working through Christ to bring the whole world back to Himself. God no longer held men's sins against them. And He gave us the work of telling and showing men this.

We are Christ's missionaries. God is speaking to you through us. We are speaking for Christ and we ask you from our hearts to turn from your sins and come to God.

II Corinthians 5:18-20

Pray for me also. Pray that I might open my mouth without fear. Pray that I will use the right words to preach that which is hard to understand in the Good News.

Ephesians 6:19

Do your best to know that God is pleased with you. Be as a workman who has nothing to be ashamed of. Teach the words of truth in the right way.

II Timothy 2:15

Preach the Word of God. Preach it when it is easy and people want to listen and when it is hard and people do not want to listen. Preach it all the time. Use the Word of God to show people they are wrong. Use the Word of God to help them do right. You must be willing to wait for people to understand what you teach as you teach them.

II Timothy 4:2

Your heart should be holy and set apart for the Lord God. Always be ready to tell everyone who asks you why you believe as you do. Be gentle as you speak and show respect.

I Peter 3:15

If a man preaches, let him do it with God speaking through him. If a man helps others, let him do it with the strength God gives. So in all things God may be honored through Jesus Christ. Shining-greatness and power belong to Him forever. Let it be so.

I Peter 4:11

Giving With A Heart Of Love

The gifts on an altar that God wants are a broken spirit. O God, You will not hate a broken heart and a heart with no pride.

Psalms 51:17

Give thanks to the Lord of All, for the Lord is good. His loving-kindness lasts forever.

Jeremiah 33:11b

Give to any person who asks you for something. Do not say no to the man who wants to use something of yours.

Matthew 5:42

Give, and it will be given to you. You will have more than enough. It can be pushed down and shaken together and it will still run over as it is given to you. The way you give to others is the way you will receive in return.

Luke 6:38

The Golden Rule

Do for other people what you would like to have them do for you.

Luke 6:31

If someone has the gift of speaking words of comfort and help, he should speak. If someone has the gift of sharing what he has, he should give from a willing heart. If someone has the gift of leading other people, he should lead them. If someone has the gift of showing kindness to others, he should be happy as he does it.

Romans 12:8

Remember, the man who plants only a few seeds will not have much grain to gather. The man who plants many seeds will have much grain to gather.

Each man should give as he has decided in his heart. He should not give, wishing he could keep it. Or he should not give if he feels he has to give. God loves a man who gives because he wants to give.

II Corinthians 9:6-7

Remember to do good and help each other.

Hebrews 13:16a

A Practical Lesson

Jesus said, "A man was going down from Jerusalem to the city of Jericho. Robbers came out after him. They took his clothes off and beat him. Then they went away, leaving him almost dead.

"A religious leader was walking down that road and saw the man. But he went by on the other side.

"In the same way, a man from the family group of Levi was walking down that road. When he saw the man who was hurt, he came near to him but kept going on the other side of the road.

"Then a man from the country of Samaria came by. He went up to the man. As he saw him, he had loving-pity on him.

"He got down and put oil and wine on the places where he was hurt and put cloth around them. Then the man from Samaria put this man on his own donkey. He took him to a place where people stay for the night and cared for him.

"The next day the man from Samaria was ready to leave. He gave the owner of that place two pieces of money to care for him. He said to him, 'Take care of this man. If you use more than this, I will give it to you when I come again.'

"Which of these three do you think was a neighbor to the man who was beaten by the robbers?"

The man who knew the Law said, "The one who showed loving-pity on him." Then Jesus said, "Go and do the same."

Luke 10:30-37

Helping Other Christians

You are the salt of the earth. If salt loses its taste, how can it be made to taste like salt again? It is no good. It is thrown away and people walk on it.

You are the light of the world. You cannot hide a city that is on a mountain.

Men do not light a lamp and put it under a basket. They put it on a table so it gives light to all in the house.

Let your light shine in front of men. Then they will see the good things you do and will honor your Father Who is in heaven.

Matthew 5:13-16

He who loves his father and mother more than Me is not good enough for Me. He who loves son or

Helping Other Christians

daughter more than Me is not good enough for Me.

He who does not take his cross and follow Me is not good enough for Me.

He who wants to keep his life will have it taken away from him. He who loses his life because of Me will have it given back to him.

Whoever receives you, receives Me. Whoever receives Me, receives Him Who sent Me.

Whoever receives a preacher who speaks for God because he is a preacher, will get the reward of a preacher who speaks for God. Whoever receives a man right with God, because he is a man right with God, will get the reward of a man right with God.

For sure, I tell you, anyone who gives a cup of cold water to one of these little ones because he follows Me, will not lose his reward.

Matthew 10:37-42

Do something to let me see that you have turned from your sins.

Luke 3:8a

The people asked him, "Then what should we do?"

He answered them, "If you have two coats, give one to him who has none. If you have food, you must share some."

Tax-gatherers came to be baptized also. They asked him, "Teacher, what are we to do?"

He said to them, "Do not take more money from people than you should."

Also soldiers asked him, "What are we to do?" He answered them, "Take no money from anyone by using your own strength. Do not lie about anyone. Be happy with the pay you get."

Luke 3:10-14

Christian brothers, if a person is found doing some sin, you who are stronger Christians should lead that one back into the right way. Do not be proud as you do it. Watch yourself, because you may be tempted also.

Help each other in troubles and problems. This is the kind of law Christ asks us to obey.

If anyone thinks he is important when he is nothing, he is fooling himself.

Everyone should look at himself and see how he does his own work. Then he can be happy in what he has done. He should not compare himself with his neighbor.

Everyone must do his own work.

Galations 6:1-5

Helping Other Christians

Because of this, we should do good to everyone. For sure, we should do good to those who belong to Christ.

Galations 6:10

My Christian brothers, our Lord Jesus Christ is the Lord of shining-greatness. Since your trust is in Him, do not look on one person as more important than another.

James 2:1

What if a person has enough money to live on and sees his brother in need of food and clothing? If he does not help him, how can the love of God be in him?

My children, let us not love with words or in talk only. Let us love by what we do and in truth.

I John 3:17-18

Reaching Out To Those In Sorrow

Come to Me, all of you who work and have heavy loads. I will give you rest.

Follow My teachings and learn from Me. I am gentle and do not have pride. You will have rest for your souls.

For My way of carrying a load is easy and My load is not heavy.

Matthew 11:28-30

In the same way, the Holy Spirit helps us where we are weak. We do not know how to pray or what we should pray for, but the Holy Spirit prays to God for us with sounds that cannot be put into words.

God knows the hearts of men. He knows what the Holy Spirit is thinking. The Holy Spirit prays for those who belong to Christ the way God wants Him to pray.

We know that God makes all things work together for the good of those who love Him and are chosen to be a part of His plan.

Romans 8:26-28

We give thanks to the God and Father of our Lord Jesus Christ. He is our Father Who shows us loving-kindness and our God Who gives us comfort.

He gives us comfort in all our troubles. Then we can comfort other people who have the same troubles. We give the same kind of comfort God gives us.

As we have suffered much for Christ and have shared in His pain, we also share His great comfort.

II Corinthians 1:3-5

The little troubles we suffer now for a short time are making us ready for the great things God is going to give us.

We do not look at the things that can be seen. We look at the things that cannot be seen. The things that can be seen will come to an end. But the things that cannot be seen will last forever.

II Corinthians 4:17-18

We are full of sorrow and yet we are always happy. We are poor and yet we make many people rich. We have nothing and yet we have everything.

II Corinthians 6:10

———————●●●●●———————

Suffering For Christ

I am sure that our suffering now cannot be compared to the shining-greatness that He is going to give us.

Romans 8:18

The things God showed me were so great. But to keep me from being too full of pride because of seeing these things, I have been given trouble in my body. It was sent from Satan to hurt me. It keeps me from being proud.

I asked the Lord three times to take it away from me.

He answered me, "I am all you need. I give you My loving-favor. My power works best in weak people." I am happy to be weak and have troubles so I can have Christ's power in me.

I receive joy when I am weak. I receive joy when people talk against me and make it hard for me and try to hurt me and make trouble for me. I receive joy when all these things come to me because of Christ. For when I am weak, then I am strong.

II Corinthians 12:7-10

You are not only to put your trust in Him, but you are to suffer for Him also.

Philippians 1:29

I want to know Him. I want to have the same power in my life that raised Jesus from the dead. I want to understand and have a share in His sufferings and be like Christ in His death.

Philippinas 3:10

Suffering For Christ

Take your share of suffering as a good soldier of Jesus Christ.

II Timothy 2:3

If we suffer and stay true to Him, then we will be a leader with Him. If we say we do not know Him, He will say He does not know us.

II Timothy 2:12

Sinful men spoke words of hate against Christ. He was willing to take such shame from sinners. Think of this so you will not get tired and give up.

In your fight against sin, you have not yet had to stand against sin with your blood.

Do you remember what God said to you when He called you His sons? "My son, listen when the Lord punishes you. Do not give up when He tells you what you must do.

"The Lord punishes everyone He loves. He whips every son He receives."

Do not give up when you are punished by God. Be willing to take it, knowing that God is teaching you as a son. Is there a father who does not punish his son sometimes?

If you are not punished as all sons are, it means

that you are not a true son of God. You are not a part of His family and He is not your Father.

Remember that our fathers on earth punished us. We had respect for them. How much more should we obey our Father in heaven and live?

For a little while our fathers on earth punished us when they thought they should. But God punishes us for our good so we will be holy as He is holy.

There is no joy while we are being punished. It is hard to take, but later we can see that good came from it. And it gives us the peace of being right with God.

So lift up your hands that have been weak. Stand up on your weak legs.

Walk straight ahead so the weak leg will not be turned aside, but will be healed.

Hebrews 12:3-13

What good is it if, when you are beaten for doing something wrong, you do not try to get out of it? But if you are beaten when you have done what is right, and do not try to get out of it, God is pleased.

These things are all a part of the Christian life to which you have been called. Christ suffered for us. This shows us we are to follow in His steps.

I Peter 2:20-21

Suffering For Christ

But even if you suffer for doing what is right, you will be happy. Do not be afraid or troubled by what they may do to make it hard for you.

Your heart should be holy and set apart for the Lord God. Always be ready to tell everyone who asks you why you believe as you do. Be gentle as you speak and show respect.

Keep your heart telling you that you have done what is right. If men speak against you, they will be ashamed when they see the good way you have lived as a Christian.

If God wants you to suffer, it is better to suffer for doing what is right than for doing what is wrong.

I Peter 3:14-17

Dear friends, your faith is going to be tested as if it were going through fire. Do not be surprised at this.

Be happy that you are able to share some of the suffering of Christ. When His shining-greatness is shown, you will be filled with much joy.

If men speak bad of you because you are a Christian, you will be happy because the Spirit of shining-greatness and of God is in you.

None of you should suffer as one who kills another

person or as one who steals or as one who makes trouble or as one who tries to be the boss of other peoples' lives.

But if a man suffers as a Christian, he should not be ashamed. He should thank God that he is a Christian.

I Peter 4:12-16

Keep awake! Watch at all times. The devil is working against you. He is walking around like a hungry lion with his mouth open. He is looking for someone to eat.

Stand against him and be strong in your faith. Remember, other Christians over all the world are suffering the same as you are.

After you have suffered for awhile, God Himself will make you perfect. He will keep you in the right way. He will give you strength. He is the God of all loving-favor and has called you through Christ Jesus to share His shining-greatness forever.

God has power over all things forever. Let it be so.

I Peter 5:8-11

Persecution May Come

Then Job stood up and tore his clothing and cut the hair from his head. And he fell to the ground and worshiped.

He said, "Without clothing I was born from my mother, and without clothing I will return. The Lord gave and the Lord has taken away. Praise the name of the Lord."

In all this Job did not sin or blame God.

Job 1:20-22

But if you will not worship, you will be thrown at once into the fire. And what god is able to save you from my hands?

Shadrach, Meshach and Abednego answered and said to the king, "O Nebuchadnezzar, we do not need to give you an answer to this question.

"If we are thrown into the fire, our God Whom we serve is able to save us from it. And He will save us from your hand, O king.

"But even if He does not, we want you to know, O king, that we will not serve your gods or worship the object of gold that you have set up."

Daniel 3:15b-18

So the king had Daniel brought in and thrown into the place where lions were kept.

Daniel 6:16a

Then Daniel said to the king, "O king, live forever! "My God sent His angel and shut the lions' mouths. They have not hurt me, because He knows that I am not guilty, and because I have done nothing wrong to you, O king."

Daniel 6:21-22

Those who have it hard for doing right are happy, because the holy nation of heaven is theirs.

You are happy when people act and talk in a bad way to you and make it hard for you and tell bad things and lies about you because you trust in Me.

Matthew 5:10-11

You will be hated by all people because of Me. But he who stays true to the end will be saved.

Matthew 10:22

Then Peter began to say to Him, "We have given up everything we had and have followed You."

Jesus said, "For sure, I tell you, there are those who

Persecution May Come

have given up houses or brothers or sisters or father or mother or wife or children or lands because of Me, and the Good News.

"They will get back one hundred times as much now at this time in houses and brothers and sisters and mothers and children and lands. Along with this, they will have much trouble. And they will have life that lasts forever in the world to come."

Mark 10:28-30

The court agreed with Gamaliel. So they called the missionaries in and beat them. They told them they must not speak in the name of Jesus. Then they were sent away.

So the missionaries went away from the court happy that they could suffer shame because of His Name.

Every day in the house of God and in the homes, they kept teaching and preaching about Jesus Christ.

Acts 5:40-42

If we are children of God, we will receive everything He has promised us. We will share with Christ all the things God has given to Him. But we must share His suffering if we are to share His shining-greatness.

Romans 8:17

But you know what I teach and how I live. You know what I want to do. You know about my faith and my love. You know how long I am willing to wait for something. You know how I keep on working for God even when it is hard for me.

You know about all the troubles and hard times I have had. You have seen how I suffered in the cities of Antioch and Iconium and Lystra. Yet the Lord brought me out of all those troubles.

Yes! All who want to live a God-like life who belong to Christ Jesus will suffer from others.

Sinful men and false teachers will go from bad to worse. They will lead others the wrong way and will be led the wrong way themselves.

II Timothy 3:10-13

My Christian brothers, you should be happy when you have all kinds of tests.

You know these prove your faith. It helps you not to give up.

James 1:2-3

Reaching Out To The World

Jesus came and said to them, "All power has been given to Me in heaven and on earth.

"Go and make followers of all the nations. Baptize them in the name of the Father and of the Son and of the Holy Spirit.

"Teach them to do all the things I have told you. And I am with you always, even to the end of the world."

Matthew 28:18-20

He said to them, "You are to go to all the world and preach the Good News to every person.

"He who puts his trust in Me and is baptized will be saved from the punishment of sin. But he who does not put his trust in Me is guilty and will be punished forever."

Mark 16:15-16

It must be preached that men must be sorry for their sins and turn from them. Then they will be forgiven. This must be preached in His name to all nations beginning in Jerusalem.

You are to tell what you have seen.

See! I will send you what My Father promised. But you are to stay in Jerusalem until you have received power from above.

Luke 24:47-49

Then Jesus said to them again, "May you have peace. As the Father has sent Me, I also am sending you."

John 20:21

But you will receive power when the Holy Spirit comes into your life. You will tell about Me in the city of Jerusalem and over all the countries of Judea and Samaria and to the ends of the earth.

Acts 1:8

PROBLEMS DURING NEW LIFE

Fear - A Natural Enemy

I looked for the Lord, and He answered me. And He took away all my fears.

Psalms 34:4

Trust in the Lord, and do good. So you will live in the land and will be fed.

Be happy in the Lord. And He will give you the desires of your heart.

Give your way over to the Lord. Trust in Him also. And He will do it.

He will make your being right and good show as the light, and your wise actions as the noon day.

Rest in the Lord and be willing to wait for Him. Do not trouble yourself when all goes well with the one who carries out his sinful plans.

Psalms 37:3-7

When I am afraid, I will trust in You.

Psalms 56:3

Fear - A Natural Enemy

The sinful run away when no one is trying to catch them, but those who are right with God have as much strength of heart as a lion.

Proverbs 28:1

The fear of man brings a trap, but he who trusts in the Lord will be honored.

Proverbs 29:25

Do not be afraid. For I have bought you and made you free. I have called you by name. You are Mine!

When you pass through the waters, I will be with you. When you pass through the rivers, they will not flow over you. When you walk through the fire, you will not be burned. The fire will not destroy you.

Isaiah 43:1b-2

When the one who hates us comes in like a flood, the Spirit of the Lord will lift up a wall against him.

Isaiah 59:19b

Just before the light of day, Jesus went to them walking on the water.

When the followers saw Him walking on the water,

they were afraid. They said, "It is a spirit." They cried out with fear.

At once Jesus spoke to them and said, "Take hope. It is I. Do not be afraid!"

Matthew 14:25-27

Peace I leave with you. My peace I give to you. I do not give peace to you as the world gives. Do not let your hearts be troubled or afraid.

John 14:27

For God did not give us a spirit of fear. He gave us a spirit of power and of love and of a good mind.

II Timothy 1:7

So we can say for sure, "The Lord is my Helper. I am not afraid of anything man can do to me."

Hebrews 13:6

There is no fear in love. Perfect love puts fear out of our hearts. People have fear when they are afraid of being punished. The man who is afraid does not have perfect love.

I John 4:18

Temptations Will Come

The man (Adam) said, "The woman (Eve) whom You gave to be with me, she gave me fruit of the tree, and I ate."

Then the Lord God said to the woman, "What is this you have done?" And the woman said, "The snake fooled me, and I ate."

Genesis 3:12-13

You must burn with fire their objects of worship. Do not want the silver or gold that is on them, or take it for yourselves. It would be a trap to you, for it is a hated thing to the Lord your God.

Do not bring a hated thing into your house. You would become hated also. But turn from it with fear and hate, for bad will come from it.

Deuteronomy 7:25-26

My son, if sinners try to lead you into sin, do not go with them.

Proverbs 1:10

Good thinking will keep you safe. Understanding will watch over you.

You will be kept from the sinful man, and from the man who causes much trouble by what he says.

You will be kept from the man who leaves the right way to walk in the ways of darkness,

from the one who is happy doing wrong, and who finds joy in the way of sin.

His ways are not straight and are not good.

Proverbs 2:11-15

Do not go on the path of the sinful. Do not walk in the way of bad men.

Stay away from it. Do not pass by it. Turn from it, and pass on.

Proverbs 4:14-15

Can a man carry fire in his arms, and his clothes not be burned?

Can a man walk on hot coals, and his feet not be burned?

Proverbs 6:27-28

A man who hurts people tempts his neighbor to do the same, and leads him in a way that is not good.

Proverbs 16:29

Temptations Will Come

He who leads good people into a sinful way will fall into his own deep hole, but good will come to those without blame.

Proverbs 28:10

He who walks with God, and whose words are good and honest, he who will not take money received from wrong-doing, and will not receive money given in secret for wrong-doing, he who stops his ears from hearing about killing, and shuts his eyes from looking at what is sinful, he will have a place on high. His safe place will be a rock that cannot be taken over. He will be given food and will have water for sure.

Isaiah 33:15-16

Watch and pray so that you will not be tempted. Man's spirit is willing, but the body does not have the power to do it.

Matthew 26:41

So do not let sin have power over your body here on earth. You must not obey the body and let it do what it wants to do.

Do not give any part of your body for sinful use. Instead, give yourself to God as a living person who has been raised from the dead. Give every part of your body to God to do what is right.

Romans 6:12-13

You have never been tempted to sin in any different way than other people. God is faithful. He will not allow you to be tempted more than you can take. But when you are tempted, He will make a way for you to keep from falling into sin.

I Corinthians 10:13

Do not let the devil start working in your life.
Ephesians 4:27

Put on the things God gives you to fight with. Then you will not fall into the traps of the devil.
Ephesians 6:11

For this reason, I could wait no longer. I sent Timothy to find out about your faith. I was afraid the devil had tempted you. Then our work with you would be wasted.

I Thessalonians 3:5

Temptations Will Come

Sinful men and false teachers will go from bad to worse. They will lead others the wrong way and will be led the wrong way themselves.

II Timothy 3:13

Because Jesus was tempted as we are and suffered as we do, He understands us and He is able to help us when we are tempted.

Hebrews 2:18

We have a great Religious Leader Who has made the way for man to go to God. He is Jesus, the Son of God, Who has gone to heaven to be with God. Let us keep our trust in Jesus Christ.

Our Religious Leader understands how weak we are. Christ was tempted in every way we are tempted, but He did not sin.

Let us go with complete trust to the throne of God. We will receive His loving-kindness and have His loving-favor to help us whenever we need it.

Hebrews 4:14-16

A man is tempted to do wrong when he lets himself be led by what his bad thoughts tell him to do.

James 1:14

So give yourselves to God. Stand against the devil and he will run away from you.

James 4:7

Keep awake! Watch at all times. The devil is working against you. He is walking around like a hungry lion with his mouth open. He is looking for someone to eat.

Stand against him and be strong in your faith. Remember, other Christians over all the world are suffering the same as you are.

After you have suffered for awhile, God Himself will make you perfect. He will keep you in the right way. He will give you strength. He is the God of all loving-favor and has called you through Christ Jesus to share His shining-greatness forever.

God has power over all things forever.

I Peter 5:8-11

But the Lord knows how to help men who are right with God when they are tempted. He also knows how to keep the sinners suffering for their wrong-doing until the day they stand before God Who will judge them.

II Peter 2:9

Life And Death

But do not eat from the tree of learning of good and bad, for the day you eat from it you will die for sure.

Genesis 2:17

The Lord kills and brings to life. He brings down to the grave, and He raises up.

I Samuel 2:6

Yes, even if I walk through the valley of the shadow of death, I will not be afraid of anything, because You are with me. You have a walking stick with which to guide and one with which to help. These comfort me.

Psalms 23:4

O Lord, let me know my end and how many days I have to live. Let me know that I do not have long to stay here.

You have made each of my days as long as a hand is wide. My whole life is nothing in Your eyes. Every man at his best is only a breath.

Every man walks here and there like a shadow. He makes a noise about nothing. He stores up riches, not knowing who will gather them.

Psalms 39:4-6

What man can live and not see death? Can he save himself from the power of the grave?

Psalms 89:48

For He knows what we are made of. He remembers that we are dust.

The days of man are like grass. He grows like a flower of the field.

When the wind blows over it, it is gone. Its place will remember it no more.

Psalms 103:14-16

No one lives for himself alone. No one dies for himself alone.

If we live, it is for the Lord. If we die, it is for the Lord. If we live or die, we belong to the Lord.

Christ died and lived again. This is why He is the Lord of the living and of the dead.

Romans 14:7-9

Our body is like a house we live in here on earth. When it is destroyed, we know that God has another body for us in heaven. The new one will not be made by human hands as a house is made. This body will last forever.

Right now we cry inside ourselves because we wish

Life And Death

we could have our new body which we will have in
heaven.

We will not be without a body. We will live in a new
body.

While we are in this body, we cry inside ourselves
because things are hard for us. It is not that we want
to die. Instead, we want to live in our new bodies. We
want this dying body to be changed into a living body
that lasts forever.

II Corinthians 5:1-5

To me, living means having Christ. To die means
that I would have more of Him.

If I keep on living here in this body, it means that
I can lead more people to Christ. I do not know which
is better.

There is a strong pull from both sides. I have a
desire to leave this world to be with Christ, which is
much better.

But it is more important for you that I stay.

Philippians 1:21-24

God planned to save us from the punishment of sin
through our Lord Jesus Christ. He did not plan for us

to suffer from His anger.

He died for us so that, dead or alive, we will be with Him.

I Thessalonians 5:9-10

It will soon be time for me to leave this life.

I have fought a good fight. I have finished the work I was to do. I have kept the faith.

There is a crown which comes from being right with God. The Lord, the One Who will judge, will give it to me on that great day when He comes again. I will not be the only one to receive a crown. All those who love to think of His coming and are looking for Him will receive one also.

II Timothy 4:6-8

It is in the plan that all men die once. After that, they will stand before God and be judged.

Hebrews 9:27

Then I saw a new heaven and a new earth. The first heaven and the first earth had passed away. There was no more sea.

I saw the Holy City, the new Jerusalem. It was coming down out of heaven from God. It was made ready like a bride is made ready for her husband.

Life And Death

I heard a loud voice coming from heaven. It said, "See! God's home is with men. He will live with them. They will be His people. God Himself will be with them. He will be their God.

"God will take away all their tears. There will be no more death or sorrow or crying or pain. All the old things have passed away."

Revelation 21:1-4

Divorce

"It has been said, 'Whoever wants to divorce his wife should have it put in writing, telling her he is leaving her.'

"But I tell you, whoever divorces his wife except if she has not been faithful to him, makes her guilty of a sex sin. Whoever marries a woman who has been divorced is guilty of a sex sin."

Matthew 5:31-32

The proud religious law-keepers came to Him. They tried to trap Him and asked, "Does the Law say a man can divorce his wife?"

He said to them, "What did the Law of Moses say?"

They said, "Moses allowed a man to divorce his wife, if he put it in writing and gave it to her."

Jesus said to them, "Because of your hard hearts, Moses gave you this Law.

"From the beginning of the world, God made them man and woman.

"Because of this, a man is to leave his father and mother and is to live with his wife.

"The two will become one. So they are no longer two, but one.

"Let no man divide what God has put together."

Mark 10:2-9

Christian brothers, I am sure you understand what I am going to say. You know all about the Law. The Law has power over a man as long as he lives.

A married woman is joined by law to her husband as long as he lives. But if he dies, she is free from the law that joined her to him.

If she marries another man while her husband is still alive, she is sinning by not being faithful in marriage. If her husband dies, she is free from the law that joined her to him. After that she can marry someone else. She does not sin if she marries another man.

Romans 7:1-3

Divorce

I have this to say to those who are married. These words are from the Lord. A wife should not leave her husband, but if she does leave him, she should not get married to another man. It would be better for her to go back to her husband. The husband should not divorce his wife.

I have this to say. These words are not from the Lord. If a Christian husband has a wife who is not a Christian, and she wants to live with him, he must not divorce her.

If a Christian wife has a husband who is not a Christian, and he wants to live with her, she must not divorce him.

I Corinthians 7:10-13

God wants you to live in peace.

Christian wife, how do you know you will not help your husband to become a Christian? Or Christian husband, how do you know you will not help your wife to become a Christian?

I Corinthians 7:15b-16

Avoiding Doubtful Situations

I was once alive. That was when I did not know what the Law said I had to do. Then I found that I had broken the Law. I knew I was a sinner. Death was mine because of the Law.

The Law is holy. Each one of the Laws is holy and right and good.

I know there is nothing good in me, that is, in my flesh. For I want to do good but I do not.

Romans 7:9, 12, 18

Be sure your love is true love. Hate what is sinful. Hold on to whatever is good.

Romans 12:9

If there is someone whose faith is weak, be kind and receive him. Do not argue about what he thinks.

Romans 14:1

The person who thinks he knows all the answers still has a lot to learn.

Since you are free to do as you please, be careful that this does not hurt a weak Christian.

I Corinthians 8:2, 9

Avoiding Doubtful Situations

Be glad you can do the things you should be doing. Do all things without arguing and talking about how you wish you did not have to do them.

In that way, you can prove yourselves to be without blame. You are God's children and no one can talk against you, even in a sin-loving and sin-sick world. You are to shine as lights among the sinful people of this world.

Take a strong hold on the Word of Life. Then when Christ comes again, I will be happy that I did not work with you for nothing.

Philippians 2:14-16

If then you have been raised with Christ, keep looking for the good things of heaven. This is where Christ is seated on the right side of God.

Keep your minds thinking about things in heaven. Do not think about things on the earth.

You are dead to the things of this world. Your new life is now hidden in God through Christ.

Christ is our life. When He comes again, you will also be with Him to share His shining-greatness.

Whatever you say or do, do it in the name of the Lord Jesus. Give thanks to God the Father through the Lord Jesus.

Colossians 3:1-4, 17

Test everything and do not let good things get away from you.

Keep away from everything that even looks like sin.

I Thessalonians 5:21-22

We are taught to have nothing to do with that which is against God. We are to have nothing to do with the desires of this world. We are to be wise and to be right with God. We are to live God-like lives in this world.

We are to be looking for the great hope and the coming of our great God and the One Who saves, Christ Jesus.

He gave Himself for us. He did this by buying us with His blood and making us free from all sin. He gave Himself so His people could be clean and want to do good.

Titus 2:12-14

Do not love the world or anything in the world. If anyone loves the world, the Father's love is not in him.

For everything that is in the world does not come from the Father. The desires of our flesh and the things our eyes see and want and the pride of this life come from the world.

The world and all its desires will pass away. But the

Avoiding Doubtful Situations

man who obeys God and does what He wants done will live forever.

I John 2:15-17

Dear Christian friends, do not believe every spirit. But test the spirits to see if they are from God for there are many false preachers in the world.

I John 4:1

Accepting Disappointments

In my fear I said, "You have closed Your eyes to me!" But You heard my cry for loving-kindness when I called to You.

Psalms 31:22

Will the Lord turn away forever? Will He never show favor again?

Has His loving-kindness stopped forever? Has His promise come to an end for all time?

Has God forgotten to be loving and kind? Has He in anger taken away His loving-pity?

I will remember the things the Lord has done. Yes, I will remember the powerful works of long ago.

Psalms 77:7-9, 11

Jesus said to them, "Do you believe now?

"The time is coming, yes, it is already here when you will be going your own way. Everyone will go to his own house and leave Me alone. Yet I am not alone because the Father is with Me.

"I have told you these things so you may have peace in Me. In the world you will have much trouble. But take hope! I have power over the world!"

John 16:31-33

We know that God makes all things work together for the good of those who love Him and are chosen to be a part of His plan.

Romans 8:28

In everything give thanks. This is what God wants you to do because of Christ Jesus.

I Thessalonians 5:18

Let us go with complete trust to the throne of God. We will receive His loving-kindness and have His loving-favor to help us whenever we need it.

Hebrews 4:16

Let us thank the God and Father of our Lord Jesus Christ. It was through His loving-kindness that we were born again to a new life and have a hope that never dies. This hope is ours because Jesus was raised from the dead.

We will receive the great things that we have been promised. They are being kept safe in heaven for us. They are pure and will not pass away. They will never be lost.

You are being kept by the power of God because you put your trust in Him and you will be saved from the punishment of sin at the end of the world.

With this hope you can be happy even if you need to have sorrow and all kinds of tests for awhile.

These tests have come to prove your faith and to show that it is good. Gold, which can be destroyed, is tested by fire. Your faith is worth much more than gold and it must be tested also. Then your faith will bring thanks and shining-greatness and honor to Jesus Christ when He comes again.

You have never seen Him but you love Him. You cannot see Him now but you are putting your trust in Him. And you have joy so great that words cannot tell about it.

You will get what your faith is looking for, which is to be saved from the punishment of sin.

I Peter 1:3-9

Difficult Situations

The Lord is the One Who goes before you. He will be with you. He will be faithful to you and will not leave you alone. Do not be afraid or troubled.

Deuteronomy 31:8

Have I not told you? Be strong and have strength of heart! Do not be afraid or lose faith. For the Lord your God is with you wherever you go.

Joshua 1:9

I looked for the Lord, and He answered me. He took away all my fears.

Psalms 34:4

We work with our hands to make a living. We speak kind words to those who speak against us. When people hurt us, we say nothing.

When people say bad things about us, we answer with kind words. People think of us as dirt that is worth nothing and as the worst thing on earth to this day.

I Corinthians 4:12-13

Difficult Situations

Every day of our life we face death because of Jesus. In this way, His life is seen in our bodies.

This is the reason we do not give up. Our human body is wearing out. But our spirits are getting stronger every day.

The little troubles we suffer now for a short time are making us ready for the great things God is going to give us forever.

We do not look at the things that can be seen. We look at the things that cannot be seen. The things that can be seen will come to an end. But the things that cannot be seen will last forever.

II Corinthians 4:11; 16-18

I have been put up on the cross to die with Christ. I no longer live. Christ lives in me. The life I now live in this body, I live by putting my trust in the Son of God. He was the One Who loved me and gave Himself for me.

Galatians 2:20

During the time Jesus lived on earth, He prayed and asked God with loud cries and tears. Jesus' prayer was to God Who was able to save Him from death. God heard Christ because Christ honored God.

Even being God's Son, He learned to obey by the things He suffered.

Hebrews 5:7-8

Christ suffered for us. This shows us we are to follow in His steps.

He never sinned. No lie or bad talk ever came from His lips.

When people spoke against Him, He never spoke back. When He suffered from what people did to Him, He did not try to pay them back. He left it in the hands of the One Who is always right in judging.

I Peter 2:21b-23

I speak strong words to those I love and I punish them. Have a strong desire to please the Lord. Be sorry for your sins and turn from them.

Revelation 3:19

Sex Sins

When evening came David got up from his bed and walked around on the roof of the king's house. From the roof he saw a woman washing herself. The woman was beautiful.

Sex Sins

So David sent someone to ask about the woman. And one said, "Is this not Eliam's daughter Bath-sheba, the wife of Uriah the Hittite?"

David sent men and took her. When she came to him, he lay with her.

II Samuel 11:2-4a

Wash me inside and out from my wrong-doing and make me clean from my sin.

For I know my wrong-doing, and my sin is always in front of me.

I have sinned against You, and You only. I have done what is sinful in Your eyes.

Psalms 51:2-4a

My son, why should you be carried away with a sinful woman and fall into the arms of a strange woman?

For the ways of a man are seen by the eyes of the Lord, and He watches all his paths.

His own sins will trap the sinful. He will be held with the ropes of his sin.

Proverbs 5:20-22

He who does sex sins with a woman does not think well. He who does it is destroying himself.

He will be hurt and ashamed, and his shame will not be taken away.

Proverbs 6:32-33

"You have heard that it was said long ago, 'You must not do sex sins.'

"But I tell you, anyone who even looks at a woman with a sinful desire of wanting her has already sinned in his heart."

Matthew 5:27-28

From the inside, out of the heart of men come bad thoughts, sex sins of a married person, sex sins of a person not married, killing other people, stealing, wanting something that belongs to someone else, doing wrong, lying, having a desire for sex sins, having a mind that is always looking for sin, speaking against God, thinking you are better than you are and doing foolish things.

All these bad things come from the inside and make the man sinful.

Mark 7:21-23

Sex Sins

Do you not know that sinful men will have no place in the holy nation of God? Do not be fooled. A person who does sex sins, or who worships false gods, or who is not faithful in marriage, or men who act like women, or people who do sex sins with their own sex, will have no place in the holy nation of God.

I Corinthians 6:9

I say this to you: Let the Holy Spirit lead you in each step. Then you will not please your sinful old selves.

The things your sinful old self wants to do are: sex sins...

Galatians 5:16, 19a

Do not be fooled. You cannot fool God. A man will get back whatever he plants!

If a man does things to please his sinful old self, his soul will be lost.

Galatians 6:7-8a

Christian brothers, we ask you, because of the Lord Jesus, to keep on living in a way that will please God. I have already told you how to grow in the Christian life.

The Lord Jesus gave us the right and the power to tell you what to do.

God wants you to be holy. You must keep away from sex sins.

God wants each of you to use his body in the right way by keeping it holy and by respecting it.

You should not use it to please your own desires like the people who do not know God.

No man should do wrong to his Christian brother in anything. The Lord will punish a person who does. I have told you this before.

For God has not called us to live in sin. He has called us to live a holy life.

The one who turns away from this teaching does not turn away from man, but from God. It is God Who has given us His Holy Spirit.

I Thessalonians 4:1-8

Marriage should be respected by everyone. God will punish those who do sex sins and are not faithful in marriage.

Hebrews 13:4

Sickness And Healing

Serve the Lord your God and He will give you bread and water. And I will take sickness from among you.

Women in your land will not lose their babies before they are born, and will be able to give birth. I will give you a full life.

Exodus 23:25-26

The Lord will take all sickness from you. He will not let any bad diseases come upon you that you have known in Egypt.

Deuteronomy 7:15

Sing for joy, O heavens! Be glad, O earth! Break out into songs of joy, O mountains! For the Lord has comforted His people. He will have loving-pity on His suffering people.

Isaiah 49:13

Jesus went over all Galilee. He taught in their places of worship and preached the Good News of the holy nation. He healed all kinds of sickness and disease among the people.

Matthew 4:23

When Jesus heard this, He said, "This sickness will not end in death. It has happened so that it will bring honor to God. And the Son of God will be honored by it also."

John 11:4

The father of Publius was sick with a stomach sickness. Paul went to see him. He prayed and laid his hands on him and the man was healed.

Acts 28:8

It is true, he was sick. Yes, he almost died, but God showed loving-kindness to him and to me.

Philippians 2:27a

Is anyone among you suffering? He should pray. Is anyone happy? He should sing songs of thanks to God.

Is anyone among you sick? He should send for the church leaders and they should pray for him. They should pour oil on him in the name of the Lord.

The prayer given in faith will heal the sick man, and the Lord will raise him up. If he has sinned, he will be forgiven.

Tell your sins to each other. And pray for each other so you may be healed. The prayer from the heart of a man right with God has much power.

James 5:13-16

PROVISIONS FOR NEW LIFE

Angels - Our Helpers

There the Angel of the Lord showed Himself to Moses in a burning fire from inside a bush. Moses looked and saw that the bush was burning with fire, but it was not being burned up.

Exodus 3:2

Then the Lord said to Moses,---

"See, I am sending an angel before you to keep you safe on the way. He will bring you to the place I have made ready.

"Listen to him and obey his voice. Do not turn against him, for he will not forgive your sins, because My name is in him.

"But if you obey his voice and do all that I say, then I will hate those who hate you and fight against those who fight against you.

"For My angel will go before you and bring you into the land of the Amorites, the Hittites, the Perizzites, the Canaanites, the Hivites and the Jebusites. And I will destroy them."

Exodus 20:22a; 23:20-23

Angels - Our Helpers

The angel of the Lord showed himself to Gideon and said to him, "The Lord is with you, O powerful soldier."

Judges 6:12

When he (Elijah) lay down and slept under the juniper tree, an angel touched him. The angel said to him, "Get up and eat."

I Kings 19:5

You alone are the Lord. You made the heavens, the heaven of heavens with all their angels. You have made the earth and all that is on it, and the seas and all that is in them. You give life to all of them, and the angels of heaven bow down to You.

Nehemiah 9:6

The angel of the Lord stays close around those who fear Him, and He takes them out of trouble.

Psalms 34:7

For He will tell His angels to care for you and keep you in all your ways.

Psalms 91:11

At once the earth shook and an angel of the Lord came down from heaven. He came and pushed back the stone from the door and sat on it.

His face was bright like lightning. His clothes were white as snow.

The soldiers were shaking with fear and became as dead men.

The angel said to the women, "Do not be afraid. I know you are looking for Jesus Who was nailed to the cross.

He is not here! He has risen from the dead as He said He would. Come and see the place where the Lord lay.

Matthew 28:2-6

The angel of the Lord came to them. The shining-greatness of the Lord shone around them. They were much afraid.

The angel said to them, "Do not be afraid. See! I bring you good news of great joy which is for all people."

At once many angels from heaven were seen, along with the angel, giving thanks to God. They were saying,

"Greatness and honor to our God in the highest heaven and peace on earth among men who please Him."

Luke 2:9-10; 13-14

Angels - Our Helpers

The head religious leader heard this. Some of the religious group who believe no one will be raised from the dead also heard of the people being healed. They became full of jealousy.

They took hold of the missionaries and put them in prison.

An angel of the Lord opened the doors of the prison in the night and let them out. The angel said to them,

"Go, stand where you have been standing in the house of God. Keep on telling the people about this new life."

Acts 5:17-20

An angel of the Lord spoke to Philip saying, "Get up and go south. Take the road that goes down from Jerusalem to the country of Gaza. It goes through the desert."

Acts 8:26

All at once an angel of the Lord was seen standing beside him. A light shone in the building. The angel hit Peter on the side and said, "Get up!" Then the chains fell off his hands.

The angel said, "Put on your belt and shoes!" He

did. The angel said to Peter, "Put on your coat and follow me."

Peter followed him out. He was not sure what was happening as the angel helped him. He thought it was a dream.

Acts 12:7-9

No one had eaten for a long time. Then Paul stood up and said to them, "Men, you should have listened to me and not left Crete. You would not have had this trouble and loss.

"But now I want you to take hope. No one will lose his life. Only the ship will be lost.

"I belong to God and I work for Him. Last night an angel of God stood by me and said, 'Do not be afraid, Paul. You must stand in front of Caesar. God has given you the lives of all the men on this ship.'

"So take hope, men. I believe my God will do what He has told me. But the ship will be lost on some island."

Acts 27:21-26

Did you not know that we are to judge angels? So you should be able to take care of your problem here in this world without any trouble.

I Corinthians 6:3

Angels - Our Helpers

Do not let anyone rob you of your prize. They will try to get you to bow down in worship of angels. They think this shows you are not proud. They say they were told to do this in a dream. These people are proud because of their sinful minds.

Colossians 2:18

But when God brought His first-born Son, Jesus, into the world, He said, "Let all the angels of God worship Him."

Hebrews 1:6

Are not all the angels spirits who work for God? They are sent out to help those who are to be saved from the punishment of sin.

Hebrews 1:14

Do not forget to be kind to strangers and let them stay in your home. Some people have had angels in their homes without knowing it.

Hebrews 13:2

I looked again. I heard the voices of many thousands of angels. They stood around the throne and around the four living beings and the leaders.

They said with a loud voice, "The Lamb Who was killed has the right to receive power and riches and wisdom and strength and honor and shining-greatness and thanks."

Revelations 5:11-12

Comfort

The Lord also keeps safe those who suffer. He is a safe place in times of trouble.

Psalms 9:9

The Lord is my rock, and my safe place, and the One Who takes me out of trouble. My God is my rock, in Whom I am safe. He is my safe-covering, my saving strength, and my strong tower.

Psalms 18:2

For He has not turned away from the suffering of the one in pain or trouble. He has not hidden His face from him. But He has heard his cry for help.

Psalms 22:24

Comfort

Wait for the Lord. Be strong. Let your heart be strong. Yes, wait for the Lord.

Psalms 27:14

The steps of a good man are led by the Lord. And He is happy in his way.

When he falls, he will not be thrown down, because the Lord holds his hand.

Psalms 37:23-24

But the saving of those who are right with God is from the Lord. He is their strength in time of trouble.

Psalms 37:39

God is our safe place and our strength. He is always our help when we are in trouble.

So we will not be afraid, even if the earth is shaken and the mountains fall into the center of the sea.

Psalms 46:1-2

Give all your cares to the Lord and He will give you strength. He will never let those who are right with Him be shaken.

Psalms 55:22

Your Word has given me new life. This is my comfort in my suffering.

Psalms 119:50

Even if I walk into trouble, You will keep my life safe.

Psalms 138:7a

He has sent me to comfort all who are filled with sorrow.

To those who have sorrow in Zion I will give them a crown of beauty instead of ashes.

Isaiah 61:2b-3a

The Lord is good, a safe place in times of trouble. And He knows those who come to Him to be safe.

Nahum 1:7

Those who have sorrow are happy, because they will be comforted.

Matthew 5:4

"Come to Me, all of you who work and have heavy loads. I will give you rest.

"Follow My teachings and learn from Me. I am gentle and do not have pride. You will have rest for

Comfort

your souls.

"For My way of carrying a load is easy and My load
is not heavy."

Matthew 11:28-30

We who have strong faith should help those who are
weak. We should not live to please ourselves.

Each of us should live to please his neighbor. This
will help him grow in faith.

Even Christ did not please Himself. The Holy
Writings say, "The sharp words spoken against you
fell on Me."

Everything that was written in the Holy Writings
long ago was written to teach us. By not giving up,
God's Word gives us strength and hope.

Now the God Who helps you not to give up and
gives you strength will help you think so you can
please each other as Christ Jesus did.

Then all of you together can thank the God and
Father of our Lord Jesus Christ.

Romans 15:1-6

We give thanks to the God and Father of our Lord
Jesus Christ. He is our Father Who shows us loving-

kindness and our God Who gives us comfort.

He gives us comfort in all our troubles. Then we can comfort other people who have the same troubles. We give the same kind of comfort God gives us.

As we have suffered much for Christ and have shared in His pain, we also share His great comfort.

II Corinthians 1:3-5

We ask you, Christian brothers, speak to those who do not want to work. Comfort those who feel they cannot keep going on. Help the weak. Understand and be willing to wait for all men.

I Thessalonians 5:14

Our Lord Jesus Christ and God our Father loves us. Through His loving-favor He gives us comfort and hope that lasts forever.

May He give your hearts comfort and strength to say and do every good thing.

II Thessalonians 2:16-17

Friends

The Lord spoke to Moses face to face, as a man speaks to his friend.

Exodus 33:11a

Friends

A man who has friends must be a friend, but there is a friend who stays nearer than a brother.

Proverbs 18:24

Do not have anything to do with a man given to anger, or go with a man who has a bad temper.

Proverbs 22:24

Do not leave your own friend or your father's friend alone, and do not go to your brother's house in the day of your trouble. A neighbor who is near is better than a brother who is far away.

Proverbs 27:10

Two are better than one, because they have good pay for their work.

For if one of them falls, the other can help him up. But it is hard for the one who falls when there is no one to lift him up.

Ecclesiastes 4:9-10

This is what I tell you to do: Love each other just as I have loved you.

No one can have greater love than to give his life

for his friends.

You are My friends if you do what I tell you.

John 15:12-14

Christian brothers, if a person is found doing some sin, you who are stronger Christians should lead that one back into the right way. Do not be proud as you do it. Watch yourself, because you may be tempted also.

Help each other in troubles and problems. This is the kind of law Christ asks us to obey.

If anyone thinks he is important when he is nothing, he is fooling himself.

Everyone should look at himself and see how he does his own work. Then he can be happy in what he has done. He should not compare himself with his neighbor.

Everyone must do his own work.

Because of this, we should do good to everyone. For sure, we should do good to those who belong to Christ.

Galations 6:1-5, 10

God Meets The Needs Of His Children

Give your way over to the Lord. Trust in Him also. And He will do it.

Psalms 37:5

Give all your cares to the Lord and He will give you strength. He will never let those who are right with Him be shaken.

Psalms 55:22

I tell you this: Do not worry about your life. Do not worry about what you are going to eat and drink. Do not worry about what you are going to wear. Is not life more important than food? Is not the body more important than clothes?

Look at the birds in the sky. They do not plant seeds. They do not gather grain. They do not put grain into a building to keep. Yet your Father in heaven feeds them! Are you not more important than the birds?

First of all, look for the holy nation of God. Be right with Him and then all these other things will be given to you also.

Do not worry about tomorrow. Tomorrow will have

its own worries. The troubles we have in a day are enough for one day.

Matthew 6:25-26, 33-34

God is able to do much more than we ask or think through His power working in us.

Ephesians 3:20

Do not worry. Learn to pray about everything. Give thanks to God as you ask Him for what you need.

Philippians 4:6

We have a great Religious Leader Who has made the way for man to go to God. He is Jesus, the Son of God, Who has gone to heaven to be with God. Let us keep our trust in Jesus Christ.

Our Religious Leader understands how weak we are. Christ was tempted in every way we are tempted, but He did not sin.

Let us go with complete trust to the throne of God. We will receive His loving-kindness and have His loving-favor to help us whenever we need it.

Hebrews 4:14-16

Keep your lives free from the love of money. Be happy with what you have. God has said, "I will never

God Meets The Needs Of His Children

leave you or let you be alone."

So we can say for sure, "The Lord is my Helper. I am not afraid of anything man can do to me."

Hebrews 13:5-6

We will receive the great things that we have been promised. They are being kept safe in heaven for us. They are pure and will not pass away. They will never be lost.

I Peter 1:4

So put away all pride from yourselves. You are standing under the powerful hand of God. At the right time He will lift you up.

Give all your worries to Him because He cares for you.

I Peter 5:6-7

He gives us everything we need for life and for holy living. He gives it through His great power. As we come to know Him better, we learn that He called us to share His own shining-greatness and perfect life.

Through His shining-greatness and perfect life, He has given us promises. These promises are of great worth and no amount of money can buy them. Through these promises you can have God's own life in you now that you have gotten away from the sinful things of the world which came from wrong desires of the flesh.

II Peter 1:3-4

We have come to know and believe the love God has for us. God is love. If you live in love, you live by the help of God and God lives in you.

I John 4:16

Jesus Teaches On The Mountain

He looked at His followers and said, "Those of you who are poor are happy, because the holy nation of God is yours.

"Those of you who are hungry now are happy, because you will be filled. Those of you who have sorrow now are happy, because you will laugh.

"You are happy when men hate you and do not want you around and put shame on you because you trust in Me.

"Be glad in that day. Be full of joy for your reward is much in heaven. Their fathers did these things to

Jesus Teaches On The Mountain

the early preachers.

"It is bad for you who are rich. You are receiving all that you will get.

"It is bad for you who are full. You will be hungry. It is bad for you who laugh now. You will have sorrow and you will cry.

"It is bad for you when everyone speaks well of you. In the same way, their fathers spoke well of the false teachers."

Luke 6:20-26

Knowing All Is Well

But God by His power gives long life to the strong. They rise again, even when they had no hope of life.

He makes them safe and gives them strength, and His eyes are on their ways.

Job 24:22-23

Do not let yourselves get tired of doing good. If we do not give up, we will get what is coming to us at the right time.

Galatians 6:9

I am sure you have heard that God trusted me with His loving-favor.

Ephesians 3:2

I am sure that God Who began the good work in you will keep on working in you until the day Jesus Christ comes again.

Philippians 1:6

I want you to know how hard I have worked for you and for the Christians in the city of Laodicea and for those who have never seen me.

May their hearts be given comfort. May they be brought close together in Christian love. May they be rich in understanding and know God's secret. It is Christ Himself.

Colossians 2:1-2

We want each one of you to keep on working to the end. Then what you hope for, will happen.

Do not be lazy. Be like those who have faith and have not given up. They will receive what God has promised them.

Hebrews 6:11-12

Knowing All Is Well

Do not throw away your trust, for your reward will be great.

You must be willing to wait without giving up. After you have done what God wants you to do, God will give you what He promised you.

Hebrews 10:35-36

But you are a chosen group of people. You are the King's religious leaders. You are a holy nation. You belong to God. He has done this for you so you can tell others how God has called you out of darkness into His great light.

At one time you were a people of no use. Now you are the people of God. At one time you did not have loving-kindness. Now you have God's loving-kindness.

I Peter 2:9-10

WISDOM FOR NEW LIFE

Where Wisdom Can Be Found

See, I (Moses) have taught you Laws just as the Lord my God told me. So you are to live by them in the land you are going to have for your own.

Keep them and do them. For this will show how wise and understanding you are. The people who will hear all these Laws will say, "For sure this great nation is a wise and understanding people."

Deuteronomy 4:5-6

"But where can wisdom be found? And where is the place of understanding?

"Man does not know its worth, and it is not found in the land of the living.

"The deep waters say, 'It is not in me.' The sea says, 'It is not with me.'

"Pure gold cannot be traded for it and it cannot be bought with silver.

"It cannot be compared in worth to the gold of Ophir, onyx of much worth, or sapphire.

Where Wisdom Can Be Found

"Gold or glass cannot be compared to it in worth and it cannot be traded for objects of fine gold.

"There is no need to say anything about coral or crystal because wisdom cannot be paid for with rubies."

Job 28:12-18

"God understands the way to wisdom, and He knows its place.

"And He said to man, 'See, the fear of the Lord, that is wisdom. And to turn away from sin is understanding.' "

Job 28:23, 28

I will show you and teach you in the way you should go. I will tell you what to do with My eye upon you.

Psalms 32:8

Then you will understand the fear of the Lord, and find what is known of God.

For the Lord gives wisdom. Much learning and understanding come from His mouth.

He stores up perfect wisdom for those who are right with Him. He is a safe-covering to those who are right in their walk.

Proverbs 2:5-7

Happy is the man who finds wisdom, and the man who gets understanding.

For it is better than getting silver and fine gold.

She is worth more than stones of great worth. Nothing you can wish for compares with her.

Long life is in her right hand. Riches and honor are in her left hand.

Her ways are pleasing, and all her paths are peace.

She is a tree of life to those who take hold of her. Happy are all who hold her near.

Proverbs 3:13-18

Keep my words and live. Keep my teachings as you would your own eye.

Tie them upon your fingers. Write them upon your heart. Say to wisdom, "You are my sister." Call understanding your special friend.

Proverbs 7:2-4

The fear of the Lord is the beginning of wisdom.

Proverb 9:10a

He who hates his neighbor does not think well, but a man of understanding keeps quiet.

Proverbs 11:12

Where Wisdom Can Be Found

One who laughs at the truth looks for wisdom and does not find it, but much learning is easy to him who has understanding.

A wise man fears God and turns away from what is sinful, but a fool is full of pride and is not careful.

Proverbs 14:6, 16

To get wisdom is much better than getting gold. To get understanding should be chosen instead of silver.

Proverbs 16:16

Sinful men do not understand what is right and fair, but those who look to the Lord understand all things.

Proverbs 28:5

For God has given wisdom and much learning and joy to the person who is good in His eyes.

Ecclesiastes 2:26a

Every time the king asked them questions that needed wise and understanding answers, he found that they knew ten times more than all the wonder-workers under his rule who used their secret ways.

Daniel 1:20

Those who are wise will shine like the bright heavens. And those who lead many to do what is right and good will shine like the stars forever and ever.

But as for you, Daniel, keep these words hidden and lock up the Book until the end of time. Many will travel here and there and knowledge will be more and more.

Many will be made pure and white and tried, but the sinners will still be sinful. None of the sinful will understand, but those who are wise will understand.

Daniel 12:3-4, 10

So be careful how you live. Live as men who are wise and not foolish.

Ephesians 5:15

In Christ are hidden all the riches of wisdom and understanding.

Colossians 2:3

Let the peace of Christ have power over your hearts. You were chosen as a part of His body. Always be thankful.

Let the teaching of Christ and His words keep on living in you. These make your lives rich and full of

Where Wisdom Can Be Found

wisdom. Keep on teaching and helping each other. Sing the Songs of David and the church songs and the songs of heaven with hearts full of thanks to God.

Whatever you say or do, do it in the name of the Lord Jesus. Give thanks to God the Father through the Lord Jesus.

Colossians 3:15-17

If you do not have wisdom, ask God for it. He is always ready to give it to you and will never say you are wrong for asking.

James 1:5

Who among you is wise and understands? Let that one show from a good life by the things he does that he is wise and gentle.

If you have jealousy in your heart and fight to have many things, do not be proud of it. Do not lie against the truth.

This is not the kind of wisdom that comes from God. But this wisdom comes from the world and from that which is not Christian and from the devil.

Wherever you find jealousy and fighting, there will be trouble and every other kind of wrong-doing.

But the wisdom that comes from heaven is first of all pure. Then it gives peace. It is gentle and willing to obey. It is full of loving-kindness and of doing good. It has no doubts and does not pretend to be something it is not.

Those who plant seeds of peace will gather what is right and good.

James 3:13-18

We know God's Son has come. He has given us the understanding to know Him Who is the true God.

I John 5:20a

THE ULTIMATE NEW LIFE

Events That Will Happen Before Christ Returns

Jesus sat on the Mount of Olives. The followers came to Him when He was alone and said, "Tell us, when will this happen? What can we look for to show us of Your coming and of the end of the world?"

Jesus said to them, "Be careful that no one leads you the wrong way.

"Many people will come using My name. They will say, 'I am Christ.' They will fool many people and will turn them to the wrong way.

"You will hear of wars and lots of talk about wars, but do not be afraid. These things must happen, but it is not the end yet.

"Nations will have wars with other nations. Countries will fight against countries. There will be no food for people. The earth will shake and break apart in different places.

"These things are the beginning of sorrows and pains.

"Then they will hand you over to be hurt. They will kill you. You will be hated by all the world because of

Events That Will Happen Before Christ Returns

My name.

"Many people will give up and turn away at this time. People will hand over each other. They will hate each other.

"Many false religious teachers will come. They will fool many people and will turn them to the wrong way.

"Because of people breaking the laws and sin being everywhere, the love in the hearts of many people will become cold.

"But the one who stays true to the end will be saved."

Matthew 24:3-13

There will be special things to look for in the sun and moon and stars. The nations of the earth will be troubled and will not know what to do. They will be troubled at the angry sea and waves.

The hearts of men will give up because of being afraid of what is coming on the earth. The powers of the heavens will be shaken.

Then they will see the Son of Man coming in the clouds with power and much greatness.

When these things begin to happen, lift up your

heads because you have been bought by the blood of Christ and will soon be free.

Luke 21:25-28

You know for sure that the day the Lord comes back to earth will be as a robber coming in the night.

When they say, "Everything is fine and safe," then all at once they will be destroyed. It will be like pain that comes on a woman when a child is born. They will not be able to get away from it.

I Thessalonians 5:2-3

Our Lord Jesus Christ is coming again. We will be gathered together to meet Him. But we ask you, Christian brothers, do not be troubled in mind or worried by the talk you hear. Some say that the Lord has already come. People may say that I wrote this in a letter or that a spirit told them.

Do not let anyone fool you. For the Lord will not come again until many people turn away from God. Then the leader of those who break the law will come. He is the man of sin.

He works against and puts himself above every kind of god that is worshiped. He will take his seat in the house of God and say that he himself is God.

Do you not remember that while I was with you, I

Events That Will Happen Before Christ Returns

told you this?

You know the power that is keeping the man of sin back now. The man of sin will come only when his time is ready.

For the secret power of breaking the law is already at work in the world. But that secret power can only do so much until the One Who keeps back the man of sin is taken out of the way.

Then this man of sin will come. The Lord Jesus will kill him with the breath of His mouth. The coming of Christ will put an end to him.

II Thessalonians 2:1-8

The Holy Spirit tells us in plain words that in the last days some people will turn away from the faith. They will listen to what is said about spirits and follow the teaching about demons.

I Timothy 4:1

You must understand that in the last days there will come times of much trouble.

People will love themselves and money. They will have pride and tell of all the things they have done. They will speak against God. Children and young people will not obey their parents. People will not be thankful and they will not be holy.

They will not love each other. No one can get along with them. They will tell lies about others. They will not be able to keep from doing things they know they should not do. They will be wild and want to beat and hurt those who are good.

They will not stay true to their friends. They will act without thinking. They will think too much of themselves. They will love fun instead of loving God.

They will do things to make it look as if they are Christians. But they will not receive the power that is for a Christian. Keep away from such people.

II Timothy 3:1-5

Christian brothers, be willing to wait for the Lord to come again. Learn from the farmer. He waits for the good fruit from the earth until the early and late rains come.

You must be willing to wait also. Be strong in your hearts because the Lord is coming again soon.

James 5:7-8

First of all, I want you to know that in the last days men will laugh at the truth. They will follow their own sinful desires.

Events That Will Happen Before Christ Returns

They will say, "He promised to come again. Where is He? Since our early fathers died, everything is the same from the beginning of the world."

But they want to forget that God spoke and the heavens were made long ago. The earth was made out of water and water was all around it.

Long ago the earth was covered with water and it was destroyed.

But the heaven we see now and the earth we live on now have been kept by His word. They will be kept until they are to be destroyed by fire. They will be kept until the day men stand before God and sinners will be destroyed.

Dear friends, remember this one thing, with the Lord one day is as 1,000 years, and 1,000 years are as one day.

The Lord is not slow about keeping His promise as some people think. He is waiting for you. The Lord does not want any person to be punished forever. He wants all people to be sorry for their sins and turn from them.

The day of the Lord will come as a robber comes. The heavens will pass away with a loud noise. The sun and moon and stars will burn up. The earth and all that is in it will be burned up.

Since all these things are to be destroyed in this way, you should think about the kind of life you are living. It should be holy and God-like.

You should look for the day of God to come. You should do what you can to make it come soon. At that time the heavens will be destroyed by fire. And the sun and moon and stars will melt away with much heat.

We are looking for what God has promised, which are new heavens and a new earth. Only what is right and good will be there.

II Peter 3:3-13

Christ's Second Coming

"This is the New Way of Worship that I will give to the Jews. When that day comes," says the Lord, "I will put My Law into their minds. And I will write it on their hearts. I will be their God, and they will be My people.

"No one will need to teach his neighbor or his brother to know the Lord. All of them will already know Me from the least to the greatest," says the Lord.

Jeremiah 31:33-34

Christ's Second Coming

Heaven and earth will pass away, but My words will not pass away.

But no one knows the day or the hour. No! Not even the angels in heaven know. The Son does not know. Only the Father knows.

When the Son of Man comes, it will be the same as when Noah lived.

In the days before the flood, people were eating and drinking. They were marrying and being given in marriage. This kept on until the day Noah went into the large boat.

They did not know what was happening until the flood came and the water carried them all away. It will be like this when the Son of Man comes.

Matthew 24:35-39

At that time the holy nation of heaven will be like ten women who have never had men. They took their lamps and went out to meet the man soon to be married.

Five of them were wise and five were foolish.

The foolish women took their lamps but did not take oil with them.

The wise women took oil in a jar with their lamps.

They all went to sleep because the man to be

married did not come for a long time.

At twelve o'clock in the night there was a loud call, "See! The man soon to be married is coming! Go out to meet him!"

Then all the women got up and made their lamps brighter.

The foolish women said to the wise women, "Give us some of your oil because our lamps are going out."

But the wise women said, "No! There will not be enough for us and you. Go to the store and buy oil for yourselves."

While they were gone to buy oil, the man soon to be married came. Those who were ready went in with him to the marriage. The door was shut.

Later the foolish women came. They said, "Sir, Sir, open the door for us!"

But he said to them, "For sure, I tell you, I do not know you!"

So watch! You do not know what day or what hour the Son of Man is coming.

Matthew 25:1-13

Heaven and earth will pass away, but My Words will not pass away.

Watch yourselves! Do not let yourselves be loaded

Christ's Second Coming

down with too much eating and strong drink. Do not be troubled with the cares of this life. If you do, that day will come on you without you knowing it.

It will come on all people over all the earth.

Be sure you watch. Pray all the time so that you may be able to keep from going through all these things that will happen and be able to stand before the Son of Man.

Luke 21:33-36

They said, "You men of the country of Galilee, why do you stand looking up into heaven? This same Jesus Who was taken from you into heaven will return in the same way you saw Him go up into heaven."

Acts 1:11

Christian brothers, we want you to know for sure about those who have died. You have no reason to have sorrow as those who have no hope.

We believe that Jesus died and then came to life again. Because we believe this, we know that God will bring to life again all those who belong to Jesus.

We tell you this as it came from the Lord. Those of us who are alive when the Lord comes again will not go ahead of those who have died.

For the Lord Himself will come down from heaven with a loud call. The head angel will speak with a loud voice. God's horn will give its sounds. First, those who belong to Christ will come out of their graves to meet the Lord.

Then, those of us who are still living here on earth will be gathered together with them in the clouds. We will meet the Lord in the sky and be with Him forever.

Because of this, comfort each other with these words.

I Thessalonians 4:13-18

We are to be looking for the great hope and the coming of our great God and the One Who saves, Christ Jesus.

Titus 2:13

Our Journey's End

"Do not let your heart be troubled. You have put your trust in God, put your trust in Me also.

"There are many rooms in My Father's house. If it were not so, I would have told you. I am going away to make a place for you.

"After I go and make a place for you, I will come back and take you with Me. Then you may be where I am."

John 14:1-3

Our Journey's End

The Holy Writings say, "No eye has ever seen or no ear has ever heard or no mind has ever thought of the wonderful things God has made ready for those who love Him."

I Corinthians 2:9

Have you not known? Have you not heard? The God Who lives forever is the Lord, the One Who made the ends of the earth. He will not become weak or tired. His understanding is too great for us to begin to know.

He gives strength to the weak. And He gives power to him who has little strength.

Even young men get tired and become weak and strong young men trip and fall.

But they who wait upon the Lord will get new strength. They will rise up with wings like eagles. They will run and not get tired. **They will walk and not become weak.**

Isaiah 40:28-31